DEADLINE

The Third Secret of Fatima

by John M. Haffert

Distributed in the U.S.A. by:
The 101 Foundation, Inc.
P.O. Box 151
Asbury, NJ 08802
Phone: (908) 689-8792
Fax: (908) 689-1957
www.101foundation.com
e-mail: 101@101foundation.com

1st printing, February 2002 — 5,000 copies
Printed in the U.S.A.
by the 101 Foundation

ISBN: 1-890137-49-9

TABLE OF CONTENTS

Contents

Important Foreword
to the Reader

THIS BOOK WAS JUST FINISHED when the sword of fire wielded by the angel of God's Justice, as depicted in the recently revealed third secret of Fatima, seemed to strike through New York's World Trade Center on September 11, 2001, piercing it like butter and bringing it to the ground.

The President of the United States declared it to be the beginning of the first war of the new millennium.

We had arrived at the deadline between God's Mercy and Justice.

I had felt an urgent need to write this book over a year before the New York disaster because many did not seem to realize that the third secret of Fatima, finally revealed in the first year of the new millennium, was a sort of ultimatum. The *actual visionary of Fatima said it referred to the annihilation of several entire nations, which we are "approaching rapidly" because of our failure to respond to the Fatima message.*

Already in these pages *we predicted that it would begin with a strike from Islam.* And God, at Fatima, had already prepared the response.

More Than Just a Wakeup Call

Pope John Paul II called September 11, 2001, "a dark day in the history of humanity..." He then continued with prayer:

"May God grant that *the faithful of the Church may be in the front line* in the search for justice, in rejection of violence, and in the commitment to be agents of peace.

"May the Blessed Virgin Mary, *Queen of Peace,* intercede for the whole world so that hatred and death may not have the last word!" (*Angelus Message*, September 30, 2001).

This was the beginning of a conflict different from any other, with unpredictable consequences. As the bombs dropped in Afghanistan, thousands rallied in neighboring Pakistan against the United States. It has fifty atomic bombs.

It is time for the whole world to awaken at last to this message given at Fatima in 1917, a message telling us that if we continue to refuse to listen to God "several *entire nations will be annihilated."*

We do not seem to want to believe this prophecy first made in 1917. We do not seem to want to accept that, when asked by the Pope what the third secret of Fatima meant, Sister Lucia replied:

"If we have not already seen the fulfillment of this last part of the prophecy (that "several entire nations will be annihilated"), *we are moving towards it day by day with giant strides."*

As Pope John Paul II has said over and over, response to the requests of Our Lady of Fatima is more urgent than ever.

The wake up call given to our nation on September 11, 2001, may be the first of many. War has been declared. Our unseen enemy has, or will have, access to nuclear weapons. Will we finally follow through in our response to the message of Fatima before it is too late?

Another Miracle Needed

The bloodless dissolution of the Soviet Union, which the Holy Father directly associated with the Fatima response, was thought an impossibility. The end to the conflict with Islam will require perhaps an even greater miracle. The initiator of this first war of the new millennium has said *there will not be peace in the West until there is peace in Palestine.* His followers, scattered in cells in many countries, willingly give their lives to kill "us."

Are there many of "us" who would make ourselves living bombs?

This new world conflict is far more complex, and far more dangerous, than it would first appear. An international Christian–Muslim conference was held in Rome a few weeks after the strike in New York. Having quickly reached the unanimous agreement that terrorist acts must be condemned, the participants moved on to consider the problems that are the cause of this new war.

Ezzedin Ibrahim (Cultural Counselor of the United Arab Emirates) said the main cause was *"an explosion of hatred, violence, and suffering in the Middle East."*

Cardinal Carlo Montini of Milan attributed it at least in part to *"excessive materialism, side by side with excessive poverty."*

Cardinal Etchegaray, former president of the Pontifical Council for Justice and Peace said: *"Religious extremism is a reaction against anti-religious extremism."* He added that economic inequalities and nationalistic ambitions fan the flames.

And what about those intelligent, well-educated, skillful young men who flew to their deaths in four hijacked jets to help destroy the nation which was aborting babies, encouraging homosexuality, and exporting pornography into the sacred precincts of Islam? In a word: a war complicated in its causes and with no foreseeable solution other than that already offered by Our Lady of Fatima.

Some Surprises

There will be some surprises in these pages, such as the suggested new role of Russia, the urgency of the new dogma requested by Our Lady of All Nations, the message of Our Lady in Kibeho which deals with pagans and Muslims and in which Our Lady said: *"The world is on the edge of catastrophe."*

Saint Padre Pio had said that Russia would be converted when there was a Blue Army member for every Communist. *Perhaps it will not be so difficult to obtain a Blue Army member for every one of the Muslim extremists.*

These extremists believe that when they give their lives to strike against us, they go straight to Heaven.

The reader may be surprised to discover in the sequel to this book, *To Shake the World,* that according to a "new" doctrine of St. Therese, Doctor of the Church, in confirmation of the teaching of another Church Doctor, St. Alphonsus Ligouri, *those who make and keep the Blue Army pledge may hope at the moment of death to go straight to Heaven.*

When enough persons have made that pledge we will see the miracle of Islamic–Christian peace. We will see the fulfillment of the final promise of Our Lady of Fatima:

"Finally my Immaculate Heart will triumph... an era of peace will be granted to *mankind.*"

The Vatican Document

To soften world reaction, when the last secret of Fatima was released by the Vatican, it was accompanied by an explanatory document issued by the Congregation for the Doctrine of the Faith. Since we quote largely from this document, we have added its complete text in an appendix to show that nothing has been quoted out of context.

Sister Lucia has indicated that *the world is almost inexorably proceeding to self destruction.* In God's Mercy the secret has been revealed *now, when it is still NOT too late!*

Perhaps the world press missed the message because *it is not the world* which can help Our Lady cause the angel's sword to be sheathed. *It is only the few generous souls.*

Two Questions

Every word of this book is written for you in the hope that you will be one of those few generous souls for whom God intends it.

In the Jubilee Year 2000, I was in my 86th year and knew I was near the end of my life. I wrote it for you *who might carry on and complete what had begun.* Time was running out.

I was diagnosed with multiple myeloma on Thanksgiving Day, 2000. It is an incurable cancer which affects the blood and bones. It was not unwelcome because I had prayed all my life that I would not die a sudden death. I had often thought of cancer as a blessing because it gives time to prepare.

I was whisked off to the hospital. Almost before I knew what was happening I was under treatment. The doctor said that even despite my age the disease, even if though incurable, was controllable.

God had given me time to finish this message to you.

How would you feel if the following conviction and understanding came to you:

1) You were suddenly and *completely convinced* that God has sent the world a warning that it is "on the edge of catastrophe—worse than the Deluge?"

2) You were also convinced that you *perfectly understood* what God required to save mankind from this catastrophe?

How I Became Convinced

Four events had convinced me:

1) In 1933, a Carmelite Brother, whom everyone recognized as a saintly man, had a vision in which the basic message of Fatima was revealed. He was told that I was the one to "make it known to the world." (See the book *The Brother and I*).

2) In 1946, at the invitation of the Bishop of Fatima, I had a lengthy interview with Sister Lucia in which she confirmed that the basic message of Fatima was what the Brother had said. We drafted a "pledge" which she affirmed contained the specific requests necessary to bring about the triumph of the Immaculate Heart and to avoid the annihilation of nations.

3) Shortly afterward, in the Chapel of the Apparitions at Fatima, the conviction came. It was a sudden *realization* of the urgency of shaking the world with this message.

4) I went to the Bishop of Fatima, showed him the pledge (the conditions of which are so simple!), and asked if he agreed that this was what was needed to fulfill the requests of Our Lady of Fatima. He answered solemnly: "You may promulgate this as coming from me."

Only One Asset Needed!

How would you feel if you had been in my place? Now, at the end of my life, *I feel greater concern than ever.*

I see the revelation of the third secret as the sign that *the time of mercy is coming to an end.* We are approaching the brink. We need at least a few more generous souls.

I decided to write this book in the hope that, as you read this, *Our Lady will give you the same conviction* I experienced by myself in the Chapel of the Apparitions of Fatima in 1946.

At first, you will probably feel as I did—helpless.

I was 27 years old. The only asset I had was a magazine which I had started during the Second World War in a crusade to obtain scapulars for our service men. With that, we started the "March of Pledges." By the end of the next year we had over a million. Only one asset is needed: It is the *totus tuus* consecration.

When Sister Lucia asked the Prioress of Pontevedra to make known the devotion of the First Saturdays, the Prioress said *there was nothing she could do.* And she did nothing.

Our Lord told Lucia shortly afterwards: *"Of herself she could do nothing, but with Me she could do it all."*

The Rest of the Story

I began this book early in the Jubilee Year with a sense that my life was rapidly coming to an end even before my cancer was diagnosed. I knew it was time to pass on the torch.

My bishop of 50 years of apostolate had insisted, in 1988, that I write the story of the apostolate because, he said, "The Blue Army is important for the Church."

An incident at his funeral convinced me that it was time to tell the rest of the story from 1988 to the present, especially of the turbulent ten years during which Pope John Paul II personally intervened to have the Blue Army institutionalized in the Church.

My wife suggested that if I was going to tell "the rest of the story," I should include some personal anecdotes.

Book Divided into Two

I did not want to mix the rest of the story with the urgency of the message of the secret. That is why this book has a sequel.

Deadline is to find those generous souls who will be convinced, by the release of the last secret, to join Our Lady in offering the Passion of Her Son to the

Father to prevent a catastrophe "worse than the Deluge" before it is too late.

The second, titled *To Shake the World*, is about passing on the torch.

I had some difficulty in deciding whether certain chapters should be in the first book or in the second. I hope the reader will read both.

The Triumph

Simeon prayed and believed that he would live to see the Savior of the World. I often prayed in that mystery of the Rosary that I would live to see the triumph of the Immaculate Heart promised at Fatima: "My Immaculate Heart will triumph. Russia will be converted and an era of peace will be granted to mankind."

I have lived to see at least its beginning, and to have a vision of what it will be. I try to explain this in the last chapter.

Showing the way, St. Grignion de Montfort foresaw and described it. I rejoice that it is rumored in Rome that he may now be declared a Doctor of the Church. He foretells even the triumph in detail.

It will be an era of such powerful saints that wondrous graces and conversions will take place. And *you can make it happen.*

Following is a summary of the two books, beginning with this one, so you may have the entire picture in brief.

Overview of First Ten Chapters

The final secret of Fatima was revealed in a truly extraordinary document from the highest level of the Church which reveals not only the secret but the essence of the message of Fatima: *devotion to the Immaculate Heart.*

It also says *to the entire Church* that *this message cannot be ignored.*

We begin by asking two questions:

1) Why was the secret revealed in this extraordinary Vatican document in 2000?

2) Why was a *"preview"* of the secret previously released at Akita in 1984 with the encouragement of the same Congregation which released the *actual* secret sixteen years later?

We find the answer in the words of Our Lady of Akita: *"So far I have been able to hold back the chastisement..."*

There is a deadline.

The next big question is: If devotion to the Immaculate Heart of Mary (as specified by Sister Lucia in the Blue Army pledge) is the answer, do we have time to explain the role of Mary even within the Church? *Many ignore Her role either deliberately or for lack of instruction.*

How will we *make known the solid basis for consecration to the Immaculate Heart*—that She is the Mother of God, Co-Redemptrix, Mediatrix, and Advocate? How can we fulfill the mandate She revealed to us at Fatima in the words: *"God wishes to establish in the world devotion to My Immaculate Heart?"*

This is the new challenge especially for the official World Apostolate of Fatima. Its Blue Army pledge contains the specific conditions given by Our Lady "to prevent this" (i.e., the annihilation of nations) and puts us on the ascent of Carmel.

The challenge cries out in a special way to the laity. The beatification of Francis and Jacinta have "canonized" Fatima's basic pledge.

The next thirteen chapters of this book, beginning with the Icon of Kazan and the possible effect on Russia, deal with the Blue Army from its decline after the dissolution of the Soviet Union to its new role after being institutionalized into the Church shortly before 2000.

Other Concerns

This is the time of Divine Mercy. It is a time when we can still expect God to intervene in a dramatic, worldwide manner to facilitate our effort.

We must address the question of reverence for the Eucharist, which is at the heart of the triumph.

It is also the special time of the *Queen of the World. She is the Lady of All Nations.*

We have a special responsibility to pray for our own nation which has been teetering between the culture of life and the culture of death. The first apparition at Fatima was that of its *national Guardian Angel,* who said, "Pray for your nation."

Finally we try to explain how near the triumph may be, and what it will be.

To Shake the World

The sequel to this book, *To Shake the World!,* is the rest of the story begun at the mandate of my bishop in 1998. It has more personal details than the earlier book titled *Dear Bishop.* It describes the loose ends, the unfinished. It is a passing on of the torch. The following is a quote from the first chapter:

> Having always been so active in trying to shake the world with the message of Fatima, I think I never had time to remember. And there were many things I *wanted* to forget. So why should I write this book now, when I am not *obliged* by obedience to my bishop?
>
> As I was considering this I noticed in the obituary column of a daily metropolitan paper that the ages of almost all who died within the previous 24 hours were younger than I. It was the same the next day, and the day after that. And this raised two questions in my mind:
>
> Did God give me health of body and mind, after 85 years of life, because I was to tell the rest of the story? If I did write it, would anybody care?

I did not know the answer to the second question. But the first recalled the words of my bishop, who I thought might still be in force even though he was now in Heaven:

"It is important... you will remember one thing and that will remind you of another. The Blue Army is important to the Church."

I decided it was time to tell the whole story in the hope that others would dare to try to shake the world crying "Wake up! You are at the brink of catastrophe, and I know what will save you!"

"The third secret of Fatima reveals an angel about to strike the world by fire. He is prevented, at least for a time, by Our Lady of Fatima.

"Mohammed wrote in the Koran that his daughter Fatima 'has the highest place in Heaven after the Virgin Mary.'

"She has told the world it has two choices: Turn to God or face annihilation of entire nations.

"Many believe the Virgin Mary, so revered by Mohammed, chose to be known today as 'Our Lady of Fatima' because She will give us the answer to this new war.

"The Vatican document which accompanied release of the secret says: '**Today the prospect that the world** *might be reduced to ashes by a sea of fire* **no longer seems pure fantasy.** *Man himself,* **with his inventions,** *has forged the flaming sword.*'"

—John M. Haffert, October 13, 2001

"With My Son, I have intervened so many times to appease the wrath of the Father. I have prevented the coming of calamities *by offering Him the sufferings of the Son on the Cross, His Precious Blood, and beloved souls who console Him* and form a cohort of victim souls. Prayer, penance and courageous sacrifices can soften the Father's anger."

—Words of Our Lady at Akita.

CHAPTER 1

Angel of Justice

Angel of Justice with fiery sword.
Pope struggles up mountain through city
half in ruins.

I N 1981, FORMER AUSTRALIAN Trappist, Lawrence Downie, skyjacked a Boeing 747 with 113 hostages on board. He forced it to land in France, doused himself in gasoline, tied gasoline canisters to his jacket, and demanded that the Pope reveal the Third Secret of Fatima.

Worldwide "crusades" were organized with petitions to the Holy See for the revelation of the Secret.

Despite the curiosity of the world and the pressures of untrusting activists, during the entire fifty-six years after the Secret was delivered in a sealed envelope to the Bishop of Fatima, four Popes in succession decided it was not the right time to make it public.[1] Finally, on May 13, 2000, just after the Pope had beatified the two youngest children of the Fatima apparitions, the Vatican's

Secretary of State on behalf of the Pope, announced:

"In order that the faithful may better receive the message of Our Lady of Fatima, the Pope has charged the Congregation for the Doctrine of the Faith with making public the third part of the Secret, after the preparation of an appropriate commentary."

Without immediately revealing the third part of the Secret, the Cardinal Secretary of State explained:

"The text contains a prophetic vision similar to those found in Sacred Scripture, which do not describe with photographic clarity the details of future events, but rather synthesize and condense, against a unified background, events spread out over time in a succession and a duration which are not specified. As a result, the text must be interpreted in a symbolic key."

Six weeks later, the Vatican revealed the third part of the Secret in a remarkable document, which explains the role of miracles and private revelations in the Church and affirms, in a definitive manner, the miracle and message of Fatima.

The third part of the Secret consists of two visions. The first is a continuation of the first

---

[1] In the memoir of Lucia of August 31, 1941, the seer wrote: "The Secret is composed of three different parts, two of which I will now reveal." The first part was a vision of Hell and prophecies involving Russia and future war. The second part was "to give us special knowledge and special love of the Immaculate Heart of Mary." The third part was first opened by Pope John XXIII in 1960. He and his successors decided not to make it known until June 26, 2000.

part of the Secret already revealed in which Our Lady had just said to the children that the dogma of the faith would always be kept in Portugal. Then, an Angel with a fiery sword appeared:

"At the left of Our Lady and a little above, we saw an Angel with flaming sword in his left hand; flashing it gave out flames that looked as though they would set the world on fire.

"But they died out in contact with the splendor that Our Lady radiated towards him from Her right hand.

"Pointing to the earth with his right hand, the Angel cried out in a loud voice: 'Penance, Penance, Penance!'"

In the accompanying document, the Cardinal Secretary of the Congregation for the Doctrine of the Faith said:

"This represents the threat of judgment which looms over the world."

The document calls it the "sign of the times"— these times.

Misunderstood in the Media

This Third Secret's symbolic vision of the Angel with the fiery sword, ready to set fire to the earth but held back by Our Lady, is a symbolic vision which, like the parables of Our Lord, may not be understood by all.

The world press, which so often looks only for the sensational, seemed to miss the true urgency and importance of the message because of one part of the explanatory document, which says:

"As far as individual events (revealed in the Secret) are described, they belong to the past.

Those who expected exciting apocalyptic
revelations about the end of the world, or
the future course of history, are bound to be
disappointed."

Elsewhere, the document explains that:

1) It is apocalyptic;

2) It is not about the end of the world, or the
future course of history, because it is of right now.

The document says:

"The Angel with the flaming sword on the
left of the Mother of God recalls similar images
in the Book of Revelation (the Apocalypse).
*This represents the threat of judgment, which
looms over the world. Today, the prospect that
the world might be reduced to ashes by a sea of
fire no longer seems pure fantasy. Man himself,
with his inventions, has forged the flaming
sword.*"

"Nations Will Be Annihilated"

In the very beginning of the document, the
Secretary of the Congregation for the Doctrine of
the Faith recalled that on May 12, 1982, Sister
Lucia wrote to the Holy Father:

"*The third part of the Secret refers to Our
Lady's words*: 'If not, (Russia) will spread her
errors throughout the world, causing wars and
persecutions of the Church. The good will be
martyred; the Holy Father will have much to
suffer; *various nations will be annihilated.*'"
(Emphasis added.)

And, Sister Lucia added:

"**If we have not yet seen the complete
fulfillment of the final part of this proph-**

ecy, we are going towards it little by little with great strides."

The Secret deals with the present world crisis in faith and morality. It is a repetition of the final words spoken by Our Lady at Fatima: "Men must cease offending God, Who is so much offended." Or else!

The Second Part

The document also states that the Secret's symbolic vision is open to more than a single interpretation.

The official documentarian of Fatima, Rev. Joaquim Alonso, CMF, felt strongly that the third part of the Secret referred to a crisis in the Church because the words spoken by Our Lady just before this Third Secret were: "The dogma of the faith will always be kept in Portugal."

The second part of the Third Secret, revealed on June 26, 2000, is as follows:

"And we saw, in an immense light that is God (something similar to how people appear in a mirror when they pass in front of it), a Bishop dressed in white (we had the impression it was the Holy Father). Other bishops, priests, men and women religious, going up a steep mountain at the top of which was a big Cross of rough-hewn trunks as of a cork tree with bark.

"Before reaching there, the Holy Father passed through a big city half in ruins. And half trembling with halting step, afflicted with pain and sorrow, he prayed for the souls of the corpses he met on his way.

"Having reached the top of the mountain, on his knees at the foot of the big Cross, he was killed by a group of soldiers who fired bullets and arrows at him. And in the same way, there died, one after another, the other bishops, priests, men and women religious, and various lay people of different ranks and positions.

"Beneath the two arms of the Cross there were two Angels, each with a crystal aspersorium in his hand, in which they gathered up the blood of the Martyrs and with it sprinkled the souls that were making their way to God."

What part of this final Secret of Fatima, made known on June 26, 2000, refers to the past? What is still to happen if we ignore the call to penance to hold back the sword of Divine Justice?

This is the challenge to the new century.

It is the challenge to bring about the promised triumph through the simple, specific requests of Fatima, which enable us each day to do the penance required so that the Angel of Justice will sheathe his flaming sword over the world.

Some feel that the "city half in ruins" represents the world struck by fire, with entire nations annihilated, if we do not enable Our Lady to hold back the Angel of Justice by fulfilling Her requests. Revealing the Secret, the Vatican document says:

"Today the prospect that the world might be reduced to ashes by a sea of fire no longer seems pure fantasy. Man himself, with his inventions, has forged the flaming sword."

Past the city half in ruins, over many corpses, the Pope climbs *"half trembling, with halting step, afflicted with pain and sorrow,"* accompanied by *"other bishops, priests, men and women religious.* He prays for the souls of the corpses he met on his way."

Could the "corpses" symbolize thousands of defected priests and religious?

The martyrdom of the Pope, with many of the devout, could still be a future reality if the warnings of Heaven continue to be ignored.[2]

Sister Lucia's View

In the Vatican document, we were given the full text of Sister Lucia's interpretation of the Secret delivered in a letter to Pope John Paul II, when His Holiness went to Fatima on May 12, 1982 to thank Our Lady for saving his life the previous May 13th.

It will be remembered that after he was shot, while recovering in the hospital, the Pope read the Third Secret for the first time. It is probable that he asked Sister Lucia for her interpretation because it is unlikely (in this writer's opinion, extremely unlikely) that Sister Lucia would have given her interpretation to the Pope unless His Holiness requested it.

To avoid any misunderstanding, the Vatican document of June 26, 2000 quoted the letter of Sister Lucia to the Pope in full, *together with a photocopy of the handwritten original.*

In this letter, Sister Lucia clearly interprets the vision of the Angel with fiery sword as an impending act of God's Justice if men do not respond to the Fatima message. She speaks of the "symbolic revelation—conditioned by whether we accept or not what the message asks of us."

Once again let us read her own words:

"The third part of the Secret refers to Our Lady's words: 'If not (that is if we do not hear

---

[2] In the first interpretation, the "arrows" shot at the Pope would be spiritual attacks. In the second, might not laser bullets have seemed to be arrows to children of 1917?

The first apparition can be shown in a single picture as above. Our Lady holds back the fiery sword of the Angel of Justice with the light from Her Sorrowful and Immaculate Heart.

The second part of the Secret would be better depicted by a motion picture, or a series of pictures. It reveals the Pope

climbing a mountain. At the top is a rough cross. He encounters many corpses on the way. He passes through a ruined city. He is killed when he reaches the top, where angels sprinkle the mountain with the blood of those who have died for the faith.

(Drawings by Sr. Mary Veronica of the Handmaids of Mary Immaculate.)

Our Lady's requests), Russia will spread her errors throughout the world, causing wars and persecutions of the Church. The good will be martyred; the Holy Father will have much to suffer; *various nations will be annihilated.*'

"If we have not yet seen the complete fulfillment of the *final part* of this prophecy, *we are going towards it little by little with great strides.*

"Let us not say that it is God who is punishing us in this way; on the contrary it is people themselves who are preparing their own punishment. In His kindness, God warns and calls us to the right path, while respecting the freedom He has given us. *Hence people are responsible.*"

It is important to note that Sister Lucia, in explaining the meaning of the Third Secret, singles out the "final part of this prophecy," which states, "various nations will be annihilated." It is the only part of the prophecy that has not yet happened. All of the other prophecies of Our Lady of Fatima, with exception of that "finally" (or "in the end"), Her Immaculate Heart will triumph, have already happened, at least in part, as in the case of the conversion of Russia.

Sister Lucia says not only that this is the meaning of the Secret. She says, *"we are going towards it little by little with great strides."*

This is a call to penance in our age like the call to penance in the time of Jonah who prophesied to the people of Nineveh that they had only forty days to repent and do penance, or perish. We do not know how many days we may have left, but whatever that deadline, we are approaching it "with great strides."

Cover of SOUL Magazine, March-April 2001, depicts the first part of the Fatima Secret. SOUL is the official voice of the Blue Army in the U.S.

To subscribe to this excellent magazine, which contains updates of Fatima and its World Apostolate, write to the Blue Army, Washington, NJ 07882, or visit them online at www.bluearmy.com.

Indeed, this is the theme of the entire Vatican document explaining the Secret (see Appendix 2). It is a reaffirmation of *the biblical call to do penance or to perish*.

The Vatican document also says that although this is "private revelation," *it is not to be ignored*, and that the main devotion of our response is to *the Immaculate Heart of Mary*.

Cannot Be Ignored

Lest the reader think we are taking words of the Vatican document out of context, we have included the entire document at the end of this book.

A large part of the document explains **why faithful Catholics should not disregard this message**. It explains the difference between public and private revelation and concludes with St. Paul: "Do not quench the Spirit, do not despise prophesying (5:19-21)."

The document quotes the Catechism of the Catholic Church:

> "Throughout the ages, there have been so-called 'private' revelations, some of which have been recognized by the authority of the Church... It is not their role to complete Christ's definitive Revelation but to help live more fully by it in a certain period of history." (No. 67)

To those who say, "we do not have to believe in Fatima," the document clearly states that private revelations, which the Church has declared authentic, "should not be disregarded." Father Louis Louchet, in his masterly book *Apparitions*, says:

> "The rationalist shrugs his shoulders when he hears of apparitions and miracles because

he does not believe and does not want to do so. He rejects God's presence in the world and is unwilling to admit that God has acted in a way requiring his own personal response. That is why, when the supernatural becomes, as it were, incarnated in a historical event, he is horrified and repelled."

The Church also is skeptical of apparitions, not for lack of faith but from fear of deception. This is *especially true of private revelations* seen as "signs of the times," containing *messages for the entire Church or for all mankind.*

Can a good Catholic deny Church-approved apparitions or messages and still remain a "good" Catholic, even though they are not obliged to believe? In the case of anyone who knows that a given miracle or apparition is authentic, at least human faith is required for that which one knows is true.

It is noteworthy that the Vatican document revealing the Secret makes this clear.

About the Future

Concerning the relation of the Secret to the future, the document states:

"In this case (of the Secret of Fatima), prediction of the future is of secondary importance. What is essential is the actualization of the definitive revelations, which concerns the individual at the deepest level. The prophetic word is a warning or a consolation, or both together. In this sense, there is a link between the charism of prophecy and the category of 'signs of the times.'

"In the private revelations approved by the Church, and therefore also in Fatima, this is the point: They help us to understand the signs of the times and to respond rightly in faith."

The Immaculate Heart

At the heart of the response asked at Fatima is devotion to the Immaculate Heart of Mary. The document explains:

"In biblical language, the 'heart' indicates the center of human life, the point where reason, will, temperament, and sensitivity converge, where the person finds his unity and his interior orientation. According to Matthew 5:8, the 'Immaculate Heart' is a heart which, with God's Grace, has come to perfect interior unity and therefore 'sees God.'

"To be 'devoted' to the Immaculate Heart of Mary means therefore to embrace this **attitude of heart, which makes the fiat, 'Your will be done,' the defining center of one's whole life**.

"It might be objected that we should not place a human being between ourselves and Christ. But then we remember that Paul did not hesitate to say to his communities: 'imitate me' (1 Cor 4:16; Phil 3;17;1 Th 1:6 and 3:7, 9). In the Apostle, they could see concretely what it meant to follow Christ. But from whom might we better learn in every age than from the Mother of the Lord?"

This last paragraph in the Vatican document concerning the Secret is especially significant. The unfolding of the message of Fatima, and the challenge of the revealed Secret to the new century, involves the intermediary role of Mary. It will be a challenge to an understanding, and affirmation, of the role of Mary in salvation history.

This is so important that we shall be speaking of it at greater length.

"People Are Responsible"

We emphasize again that this remarkable document on the Third Secret of Fatima, in affirming the miracle and message of Fatima with all its prophecies, declares in the words of Sister Lucia herself:

"If we have not yet seen the complete fulfillment of the final part of this prophecy, we are going towards it little by little with great strides."

She adds that people themselves are preparing their own punishment and therefore, "people are responsible." If we are to avoid the flaming sword of God's Justice from setting fire to the earth, we must do as Our Lady at Fatima has asked.

The Third Secret's symbolic vision of the Angel with the fiery sword, ready to set fire to the earth but held back by Our Lady, is a message especially for those who can understand and who will respond. It is a challenge most especially to those already consecrated to the Immaculate Heart in one apostolate or another, but most especially in the official, Church-recognized Apostolate of Fatima.

This is the special responsibility of its leaders.

All can be summed up in those simple words of the October 13, 1977 letter of Pope John Paul II, that the importance of Fatima is not in the miracles but in the fact that Fatima indicates the specific response necessary to save mankind from self-destruction.

An Angel of Divine Justice stands ready to set fire to the earth. In His Mercy, God sends "the Mother" to hold back the fiery sword. *She comes at*

Fatima in a miracle of fire, which caused tens of thousands to think it was the end of the world. And She tells us what we must do to cause the Angel of Justice to sheathe the sword.

An artist's depiction of the Secret, published by the Postulation for the canonization of Blessed Francisco and Jacinta.

CHAPTER 2

Message for the New Century

Why the Secret was kept for so long.

S PEAKING TO THE HUNDREDS of thousands present at Fatima for the beatification of the children, and to millions watching by television, the Cardinal Secretary of State said some parts of the Secret, already largely fulfilled, continue now:

> "Attacks against the Church and against Christians, together with the burden of suffering which they involve, tragically continue. Even if the events to which the third part of the Secret of Fatima refers now seem part of the past, *Our Lady's call to conversion and penance*, issued at the beginning of the twentieth century, *remains timely and urgent today.*
>
> "The Lady of the message seems to read the signs of the times—the signs of our time—with special insight... The insistent invitation of Mary Most Holy to penance is nothing but

the manifestation of Her maternal concern for the fate of the human family, in need of conversion and forgiveness."[3] (Emphasis added.)

Our Lady Also Prepared the Way

This statement prepared the way for the world to learn the third part of the Secret.

Our Lady Herself had already prepared the Church by Her message in Akita, Japan, which was released in a pastoral letter by the bishop of the diocese in which She appeared in March 1984.

Books, which appeared in Japan, and then translated and published in other nations, helped spread the word within the Church.[4] (The basic message was published in SOUL Magazine, the official voice of the Blue Army, in 1988.)

Many reacted incredulously.

Even though the Prefect of the Sacred Congregation of the Doctrine for the Faith (Cardinal Ratzinger) said the message of Akita was similar to the Third Secret of Fatima, the world did not seem ready to hear the warning of "an Angel with

---

[3] Message of John Paul II for the 1997 World Day of the Sick, No. 1, in *Insegnamenti*, vol. xix/2, 1996, pg. 561.

[4] One of the first books about Akita was written by Father Shimura, President of the Blue Army in Japan and rector of the Cathedral in Tokyo. The basic "source" work was written by Father Yasuda, spiritual director of the convent of the apparitions. Then editor of SOUL Magazine, I wanted to write a new book based on the works of Fr. Shimura and Father Yasuda. When I asked the advice of Bishop Ito of Akita, His Excellency asked me first to translate the Yasuda book in its entirety. It was published in 1989: *Akita, the Tears and Message of Mary* (202 pp). I later wrote a smaller book, *The Meaning of Akita*, published in the same year, which contains all the words spoken in the Akita apparitions.

a flaming sword...flames that looked as though they would set the world on fire."

Of special meaning in the statement of Cardinal Sodano on May 13 at Fatima are the words: *"Our Lady's call* to conversion and penance, issued at the beginning of the twentieth century, remains *timely and urgent today."*

To grasp the full picture, it is important to understand why Cardinal Ratzinger said that keeping the message Secret until 2000 was "a matter of prudence."

Why a Secret So Long

In the first part of the Secret, Our Lady said (after showing the children a vision of Hell):

"You have seen Hell where the souls of poor sinners go. To save them, God wishes to establish in the world devotion to My Immaculate Heart. If what I say to you is done, many souls will be saved and there will be peace. The war (World War I) is going to end. But if people do not cease offending God, a worse one will break out during the pontificate of Pius XI.[5]

"When you will see a night illumined by an unknown light, know that this is the great sign given by God that He is about to punish the world for its crimes by means of war, famine and persecutions of the Church and of the Holy Father.

"To prevent this, I shall come to ask for the consecration of Russia to My Immaculate Heart and the Communions of Reparation on the First

---

[5] By "coincidence," Father Eugenio Pacelli was ordained a bishop on May 13, 1917, the day of the first apparition of Fatima. He became Pope Pius XII, who succeeded Pius XI just after the beginning of the Second World War with Hitler's march into Austria.

Saturdays. If My requests are heard, Russia will be converted and there will be peace. If not, she will spread her errors throughout the world, causing wars and persecutions of the Church. The good will be martyred. The Holy Father will have much to suffer. Several nations will be annihilated.

"Finally, My Immaculate Heart will triumph. The Holy Father will consecrate Russia to me and she will be converted, and an era of peace will be granted to the world."

Some parts of this Secret were gradually made known even before release of the entire text.

On the very day of the miracle (October 13, 1917), the children said that the First World War would soon end. It was on that same day that the first American troops landed in France; the war ended within a year.

Also when the "unknown light" was seen over Europe, giving the impression that all the nations of Europe were on fire, Lucia made known to the

Pilgrims fill the Cova of Fatima on May 13, 2000, as they and the world hear for the first time that the Pope has ordered the release of the third and last Secret of Fatima.

bishop that this was the "great sign" that the Second World War was about to begin.

Secrecy Was Necessary

There are two obvious reasons why God willed that the first two parts of the Secret should be kept until 1942:

1) The prophecy of a "more terrible war" (naming the Pope in whose time it would begin), and the prophecy that "several entire nations will be annihilated," could have had an adverse effect on the canonical inquiry about the authenticity of the Fatima miracle and message.

2) These prophecies would not have been as believable even until 1942. Even until a few years later when the atom bomb was first exploded in Japan, it would have been difficult to believe that "several entire nations will be annihilated."

It is because these prophecies seemed so "unbelievable" that if they had not been kept Secret, the very message of Fatima might never have been made known. We can deduce this from what happened in Akita.

Because of the severity of the message revealed at Akita, the Bishop at first decided not to make it known. Only after repeated signs from Heaven, and after three trips to Rome to consult with the Sacred Congregation for the Doctrine of the Faith, did the Bishop finally publish the message after assurance by Cardinal Ratzinger, Prefect of the Congregation which had custody of the Fatima Secret, that the Akita message was in keeping with the third part of the still-kept Fatima Secret.

It was necessary, in the plan of God's Providence, that the Church would have determined beyond doubt (based largely on the miracle of October 13, 1917) that this message was a message from God before revealing these prophecies which challenge the world in the same words spoken over a hundred years before at Lourdes: "Penance! Penance! Penance!"

Vision of Hell Related to Chastisement

While we can see the prudence of withholding for a time such prophecies (about Russia, the war, and the annihilation of nations) until they were more believable, why was the vision of Hell also kept Secret?

A first reason might be that it was especially in the second half of the last century that the world was losing its sense of sin and belief in Hell. But also, it was because the vision of Hell (with Our Lady's most important words, "If what I say to you

Bishop Ito, as Bishop of the Diocese of Akita, approved the apparitions of Our Lady of Akita on April 22, 1984. On advice of Cardinal Ratzinger, His Excellency requested ratification by the Episcopal Conference of Japan, which came about November 29, 1990.

is done, many souls will be saved") is related to the impending chastisement.

The loss of many souls is probable through fiery chastisement if that exhortation of Our Lady continues to be ignored.

Also, *only after the fulfillment of the earlier prophecies would the world better understand the importance of devotion to the Immaculate Heart of Mary and of making Communions of Reparation on First Saturdays.*

If we do not bring an end to the tidal wave of evil by fulfilling Our Lady's requests, God's Justice and Mercy will end it by fire. "Sin is the cause of war," Our Lady said. At the same time, She predicted further wars and annihilation of entire nations, if the tidal wave of sin does not stop.

The Second Part

The "second part" of the Secret, of which we hear far too little, was actually revealed before the first part. However, both parts are intertwined.

In Lucia's own words, *"the second part refers to devotion to the Immaculate Heart of Mary."* She explains what happened, as light streamed from Our Lady's Heart:[6]

> "I think that the main purpose of this light was to infuse us with special knowledge and love for the Immaculate Heart of Mary...
>
> "From that day onwards, our hearts were filled with a more ardent love for the Immaculate Heart of Mary.

---

[6] *Her Own Words to the Nuclear Age*, pg. 167, available from the 101 Foundation.

"From that time on, whenever we spoke of this, Jacinta said to me: 'The Lady said that Her Immaculate Heart will be your refuge and the way that will lead you to God. Don't you love that? Her Heart is so good. How I love It!'

"As I explained earlier, in the July Secret, Our Lady told us that God wished to establish in the world devotion to Her Immaculate Heart; and that to prevent a future war, She would come to ask for the consecration of Russia to Her Immaculate Heart and for Communions of Reparation on the First Saturdays.

"From then on, whenever we spoke of this among ourselves, Jacinta (who at the time was considered too young to receive Communion) said: 'I am so grieved not to be able to receive Communion in Reparation for the sins committed against the Immaculate Heart of Mary!'"

Good Reason for Secrecy

Even when she finally felt compelled to reveal the first two parts of the Secret, Sister Lucia wrote:

"My repugnance in making this known is so great that, although I have before me the letter in which Your Excellency orders me to write everything I can remember (and I feel interiorly convinced that this is indeed the hour that God has chosen for my doing this), I still hesitate and experience a real inner conflict, not knowing whether to give you what I have written or to burn it... For me, keeping the Secret has been a great Grace. What would have happened... Who knows but that I might have caused such a confusion of ideas as even to spoil the work of God. For this reason, I give thanks to the Lord. I know that He does all things well."[7]

---

[7] Ibid.

In retrospect, we can see that it was most fitting for the first parts of the Secret to be kept until the authenticity of Fatima had already been confirmed by the Church, when the prophecies contained in the Secret (about Russia, the Second World War, and the annihilation of nations) were believable.

It would certainly have seemed incredible in 1917, when "Holy Mother Russia," defeated in World War I and engulfed in the bloodshed of the Bolshevik Revolution, would become "atheist Russia" and would "spread her errors throughout the entire world."

But by 1941, the prophecy of Our Lady about Russia was already coming true.

In 1942, the year after this prophecy was made known, responding to the request of Our Lady of Fatima, Pope Pius XII consecrated the world to the Immaculate Heart of Mary with special reference to "that nation where Our Lady's Icon is hidden, awaiting a better day."

The Third Part

The only part of the message still very difficult to believe in 1942 was that *"several entire nations will be annihilated."* But just three years later, the first atomic bombs were dropped in Japan. *The terrible, almost unbelievable prophecy was now believable.*

Then appearing in Japan, on the anniversary of the Fatima miracle (October 13) in 1973, Our Lady explained the meaning of those words. The Bishop of Akita in Japan made the message public in a pastoral letter on March 27, 1982.

Appearing in a transformed image of Our Lady of All Nations, Our Lady said:

"Many men in this world afflict the Lord. If men do not repent and better themselves, the Father will inflict a terrible punishment on all humanity.

"It will be a punishment worse than the Deluge, such as one will never have seen before. Fire will fall from the sky and will wipe out a great part of humanity... The survivors will find themselves so desolate that they will envy the dead."

From the very contents of this message, which the Prefect of the Sacred Congregation for the Doctrine of the Faith said conforms to the Third Secret of Fatima, *we can see that it would not have been prudent for it to have been announced by the Pope until it could be done in a manner which would make it clear without harm to the Church.*

Sister Lucia herself wrote in 1941, as we mentioned above, that it might have caused "such a confusion of ideas as even to spoil the work."

Without sufficient preparation, reaction of many would have been not only one of confusion, but perhaps also of incredulity and even ridicule.

As Sister Lucia said in 1941, she was glad it was Secret until the Lord would decide to have it revealed. She said: "I give thanks to the Lord (for keeping the Secret). I know that He does all things well."

For Special Souls

When Pope John Paul II decided to make the entire Secret public according to the announcement by Cardinal Sodano at Fatima on May 13, 2000, it was also decided that, taking advantage of the worldwide curiosity created by the Secret, the Church would explain the message of Fatima as "the most prophetic of modern apparitions," and would explain clearly the difference between public and private revelation.

We must conclude that the vision of the Angel with the fiery sword, about to set fire to the earth, was not to be bluntly announced to an incredulous, doubting world. It was to be "interpreted in symbolic key" for those who will respond in faith. The more complete revelation, through the apparition in Japan as confirmed by the Prefect of the Congregation of the Doctrine of the Faith, enables devout souls to respond not with panic but with faith.

The response to this message, which can prevent further wars and even destruction of entire nations, is the great challenge in the new century to persons of faith.

Is that not why it was revealed in the middle of the Jubilee Year, opening the new millennium?

It involves devotion to the Immaculate Heart of Mary beginning with the "specific response" of the pledge promoted by the World Apostolate of Fatima (the Blue Army) and flowering in the total consecration exemplified in the life and writings of Pope John Paul II himself.

Many Other Confirmations

Some twenty years after the apparitions of Fatima, not long before Sister Lucia put the Third Secret in a sealed envelope for the Pope, it was revealed to Saint Faustina:

> "I saw the Mother of God, with Her breast bared and pierced with a sword. She was shedding bitter tears and shielding us against God's terrible punishment.
>
> God wants to inflict terrible punishment on us, but He cannot because the Mother of God is shielding us.

Horrible fear seized my soul... If it were not for the Mother of God, all our efforts would be of little use.

I see that I am a drop before the wave of evil. How can a drop stop a wave? Oh, yes! A drop is nothing of itself, but... Your Omnipotence can do all things."[8]

Let us pray that our reaction to the revelation of the Third Secret of Fatima will be like that of Saint Faustina when Our Lady Herself revealed it to her. Our Lady said She has been able to hold back the chastisement because of the response of a few generous souls who form a cohort with Her. She said She has been able to hold it back "so far."

And "so far" means until now.

Saint Faustina

---

[8] From the *Diary of Saint Faustina*, #686.

CHAPTER 3

How Much Time?

Our Lady has been holding back
the chastisement, "SO FAR."

A S WE SAID, the release of the Third Secret of Fatima prematurely could have resulted not only in confusion, but perhaps also incredulity and even ridicule. This became evident in the secular as well as the Catholic press when revelation of the Third Secret was announced on May 13, 2000.

A major newspaper of England, *The Sunday Telegraph,* asked the question: "What will the disclosures of the Third Secret have on believers?" And the answer was to the point:

"Many Catholics in this country *will feel vaguely embarrassed.* For many, the story of Fatima is too exotic."[9]

Some papers took no notice whatever. The world did not seem ready for a message from Heaven.

---

[9] *The Sunday Telegraph*, May 14, 2000, pg. 22.

But the seriousness of this message from Heaven challenges those who know, and most *especially challenges those entrusted with the responsibility of the message*. It is the challenge to find enough generous souls to weigh down the balance of Divine Justice in time to save a sinning world by Grace rather than by fire.

The task will be made more difficult because of the "embarrassment," in today's "scientific" and unbelieving world, of being members of a Church that believes in miracles and messages from Heaven.

Sister Lucia called it "an ongoing process."

But this great challenge to bring enough souls into the refuge of the Immaculate Heart of Mary before God may find it necessary to purify the world by fire is reaching a deadline.

We do not know the time limit. But we know it will depend on a believing and courageous few who know that no matter how daunting it may seem, victory has been promised.

God May Intervene Again

In His Divine Mercy, God will not abandon us to chastisement just because we have ignored the Miracle of the Sun and the Great Sign of 1938.[10]

Sooner or later, we can hope that every person on earth will experience an illumination of conscience in what St. Margaret Mary called "God's final effort to wrest mankind from the dominion of Satan."[11]

---

[10] See the author's books *Meet the Witnesses* and *Her Own Words*. The Great Sign, prophesied in the first part of the Fatima Secret, was seen over about one fourth of the world on the night of January 24-25, 1938, causing millions to think the world was on fire.

[11] See the author's book *The Great Event*, published by the 101 Foundation in 2000.

The Holy Father has described response to the Fatima message as the saving of mankind from self-destruction. This was the expression used by the Pope in the historic letter of October 13, 1997, in which His Holiness said the greatness of Fatima lies in the fact that Our Lady has given us "the specific response" necessary "to save mankind from self-destruction." And the first two sentences of his prayer of consecration to the Immaculate Heart of Mary, made after he had read the Fatima Secret, were:

"From famine and war, deliver us.

"From nuclear war, from incalculable self-destruction, deliver us."

The Great Hope

What must be of great concern is that so many, even within the Church, do not know or understand the message of consecration to the Immaculate Heart of Mary, which is the basis of the "specific response."

Outside the Church, there is an almost total and disheartening ignorance, so great that it might cause us to wonder how the few "apostles" of the Fatima message might ever overcome it.

But the Fatima message offers a very real hope. It ends with the words: "Finally My Immaculate Heart will triumph...an era of peace will be granted to mankind."

We will speak of this hope in the following pages, a hope that lies in *the enormous power* of the prayer of souls who will carry consecration to the Immaculate Heart of Mary to the limit—to TOTAL consecration. We will see an extraordinary example of that power in new saints like St. Faustina, the messenger of Divine Mercy.

The number of those souls who have so far enabled Our Lady to hold back the chastisement will continue to grow. The Angel of Akita said:

"Many men in this world afflict the Lord. Our Lady awaits souls to console Him... The Rosary is your weapon. Say it with care and more often for the intention of the Pope, of bishops and priests.

"You must not forget those words (of Our Lady). The Blessed Virgin prays continually for the conversion of the greatest possible number and weeps, hoping to lead to Jesus and to the Father souls offered to Them by Her intercession. For this intention, and to overcome exterior obstacles, achieve interior unity. Form a single heart. Let believers lead lives more worthy of believers! *Pray with a new heart.*

"Attach great importance to this day (First Saturday) for the glory of God and of His Holy Mother. With courage spread this devotion among the greatest number."

In the light of those words of the Angel, the words of Our Lady Herself take on a special poignancy:

"Many men in this world afflict the Lord. I desire souls to console Him to soften the anger of the Heavenly Father. I wish, with My Son, for souls who will repair by their suffering and their poverty for the sinners and ingrates."

A Message of Divine Mercy

Then, after repeating that God is about to inflict "a great chastisement" on mankind, Our Lady said:

"With my Son, I have intervened so many times to appease the wrath of the Father. I have prevented the coming of calamities by offering Him the sufferings of the Son on the Cross, His Precious Blood, and beloved souls who console Him and form a cohort of victim souls."

Since the canonization of St. Faustina on April 30, 2000, many more will now know that *this is the message of Divine Mercy.*

St. Faustina said that when we offer the Passion of Jesus to the Father in reparation for our sins and those of the whole world, *rays of Mercy flood the world.* When we make the offering *in union with His Mother at the foot of the Cross, enormous power is unleashed to drive back the tidal wave of evil.* We shall be speaking of this in greater depth.

Meanwhile, we wonder once again why, despite the great Miracle of the Sun and the affirmation of Fatima by one Pope after the other, we seem to blind our eyes to this message of hope, this alternative to mankind's self-destruction.

Why Has It Been Ignored?

The first part of the message of Fatima speaks of *the annihilation of entire nations.* This awesome prophecy has been repeated and clarified in the third part and at Akita:

"It will be worse than the Deluge... The survivors will find themselves so desolate that they will envy the dead." But so far, Our Lady has been able to hold it back.

The people of the world, who have ignored the message of Fatima for more than half a century, are reminded at the beginning of the new millennium that if the requests continue to be ignored, what was prophesied in 1917 is going to happen: "*several entire nations will be annihilated.*"

At the same time, they are told how it can be prevented. Sister Lucia, at the direction of Our Lord and/or her confessor, wrote to the Holy Father repeatedly of the terrible events about to come but which could be prevented if the First Saturday devotion was promoted and put into practice. As late as June 20, 1939, a year and a half after the "Great Sign" was seen all over Europe, she wrote:

> "Our Lady promised to defer the calamity of war if this devotion were to be propagated and put into practice. We see Her holding back this punishment as much as efforts are being made to propagate the devotion. But I am afraid we do not do as much as we can and God, being displeased, *will withdraw the arm of His Mercy and let the world be devastated by that punishment which will be horrible, horrible.*"[12]

Those words should be burned into our hearts now, and especially into the hearts of those entrusted with the responsibility of making the message of Fatima known and practiced.

It is because *"we do not do as much as we can"* that "God, being displeased, will withdraw the arm of His Mercy."

Time is LIMITED

Towards the end of the last century, we were repeatedly told that it was the time of Mercy. As we have already suggested, that time of Mercy, like all time, *has a limit.* If we do not respond, as happened before, God *"will withdraw the arm of His*

---

[12] *Documentos*, ix.

Mercy and let the world be devastated by that punishment which will be horrible, horrible."

The catastrophes of Bosnia and Rwanda, *where Our Lady had appeared ten years before the massacres* with Her appeal for prayer and penance, witness to *the inevitable effect of ignoring God's warnings.*[13]

It is too late for hundreds of thousands in the Balkans. It is too late for hundreds of thousands in Rwanda, where over 800,000 perished mostly by beheading as Our Lady predicted.[14]

Will it soon be too late for us?

I remember when the bishop in Rwanda encouraged me to translate the messages into English. I put it off, even though Our Lady had said: "I am concerned not only for Rwanda, or for Africa, *but for the whole world. The world is on the edge of catastrophe."*

I put it off, thinking: *"there is plenty of time... I will wait until the bishop actually approves the apparitions."* I wanted to avoid being categorized as a promoter of "unapproved" apparitions.[15]

---

[13] See the author's book *Too Late?*, published by the 101 Foundation.

[14] The dimensions of the Rwanda tragedy are almost beyond comprehension. Originally, it was thought that about 500,000 were slaughtered in that small and largely Christian country, but during the trials in the International Court, the number was corrected to 800,000, and later to one million.

[15] This "accusation" had been leveled at me and at the 101 Foundation, over which I had no control. It was as though to speak of apparitions before Church approval was anathema. If I refer to any "unapproved" apparitions in this book, it is only by reference or because of indication of approval by the local bishop, as in the case of the apparitions in Kibeho.

The approval came in good time.[16] But for me it was too late to write about it, as it was also too late for that little nation in which a large part of its entire population was slaughtered, and many of those who survived have envied the dead.

Could Have Been Prevented

Sister Lucia wrote in June of 1939, just a few months before the Second World War: "Our Lady promised *to defer the calamity... We see Her holding back this punishment.*"

Only several MONTHS remained after that message before the outbreak of the Second World War! Even *then*—even on the very eve of the bloodiest war in history, *it could have been prevented.*

Our Lady was "holding back this punishment," waiting for our response.

But within less than a year, it was too late.

To spread the message of Fatima effectively is not only an urgent and great challenge to the new century, it is also a great responsibility. Saint Faustina said:

"The Mother of God said to me: 'Oh, how pleasing to God is the soul that follows faithfully the inspirations of His Grace! I gave the Savior to the world; as for you, *you have to speak to the world* about His great Mercy and prepare the world for the Second Coming of Him Who will come, not as a merciful Savior, but as a just Judge. Oh, how terrible is that day!... The angels tremble before it. Speak to

---

[16] Public cult at Kibeho was authorized in a pastoral letter by the bishop of the diocese on August 15, 1988. The book in question is *Les Apparitions de Kibeho,* by Father Gabriel Maindron, published in Paris by O.E.I.L. (12, rue du Dragon).

souls about this great Mercy while it is still the time for Mercy. *If you keep silent now, you will be answering for a great number of souls on that terrible day.'"*

We deserve God's chastisement, but in His Mercy, He sends Our Lady of Mercy "to prevent this."

Blessed Jacinta exclaimed: "In His Mercy, He has entrusted the peace of the world to Her!"

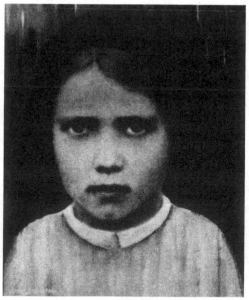

Blessed Jacinta

CHAPTER 4

The Great Challenge

The Secret becomes a new battle cry to save mankind from self-destruction.

GOD HAS ALREADY intervened again and again to draw mankind back from the edge of catastrophe—to "wrest mankind from the dominion of Satan" in the "final effort," which began with the revelations of the Sacred Heart, to be completed at Fatima in the revelations of the Immaculate Heart of His Mother.[17]

The attention drawn to the Third Secret of Fatima on May 13, 2000 cries out especially to persons of faith. Many have reacted with indifference, embarrassment, or even ridicule.

But, in many quarters, there was a dawn of realization of the great importance of the Fatima message as, in the words of Pope John Paul II,

---

[17] Words in quotation marks were spoken by Saint Margaret Mary Alacoque. See author's book *God's Final Effort*.

"the alternative to mankind's self-destruction." For example, the prominent British author, Piers Paul Read, saw the disclosures of the Third Secret as "very significant," and as a call to look at the message of Fatima more earnestly.

"As another prophecy of Fatima has been shown to have been fulfilled," he said, "it validates the other visions. We must now go back and examine them. *It is extremely powerful* and it should give people *pause for thought.*"[18]

This reaction from many who were previously indifferent to the message of Fatima *creates a new opportunity for the Fatima Apostolate all over the world.*

Before the dissolution of the Soviet Union, the battle cry of the Fatima Apostolate was in the words and promise: "Russia will be converted."

Now we have the new and more powerful battle cry of the Third Secret: *to join with Our Lady to shield the world from the Angel's flaming sword of God's Justice.*

It is the call to save the world by Grace rather than by fire, through the specific response given to us at Fatima.

Special Responsibility

Obviously, as we have already said, this major responsibility now falls especially on the Blue Army, a fifty-year-old movement recognized in the Church as "the World Apostolate of Fatima."

The Bishop of Akita himself came to the Blue Army Center in Washington, NJ, and made a spiritual affiliation between the Blue Army Sisters, the

---

[18] *The Sunday Telegraph*, May 14, 2000, pg. 22.

Handmaids of Mary Immaculate, and his Handmaids of the Holy Eucharist, the community involved in the apparitions and miracles of Akita. When asked if there should be a new apostolate to spread the final message of the Third Secret as it was revealed by Our Lady at Akita, the bishop said: "No. *It is the task of the Blue Army.*"

This is a responsibility and challenge not only for the leaders of the Apostolate but also for those twenty-five million who made the Blue Army pledge before the dissolution of the Soviet Union. They are now challenged to enter more deeply, and to live more completely, their consecration to the Immaculate Heart of Mary and to make it known to others.

Each one who KNOWS the message has a special *responsibility* to fulfill it, and to cause it to be fulfilled by others.

The alternative is mankind's self-destruction.

We Are At the End of the Signs

The message of Akita before the revelation of the Secret of Fatima had been largely ignored.[19] But when the revelation of the Secret was announced in the presence of the Pope at Fatima on May 13, 2000, the world was told that *the results of atheism "tragically continue" and "Our Lady's call...remains timely and urgent..."*

We were warned in the last century by three great signs unprecedented in history: The Miracle

---

[19] The new leadership of the Blue Army in the United States did not at once accept the Akita message, but the apostolate in the Philippines, Korea, and Japan responded after the apparitions and miracles had been declared to be supernatural.

of the Sun, the "Great Sign" of 1938, and the predicted wars culminating in the first use of atomic bombs. *The world ignored the signs and endured the bloodiest century in history.*

Now we have additional signs *of fulfilled prophecies*: Atheism spread from Russia throughout the world, persecution (which was severe behind the Iron Curtain and is still severe in China and elsewhere), suffering of the Holy Father, the "Great Sign," the Second World War, and the dissolution of the Soviet Union following the Collegial Consecration.

It appears that we are at the end of the Fatima signs. "The world is on the edge of catastrophe." (Our Lady's words in Rwanda.)

In 1993, only seven years before the new millennium, Sister Lucia said, "The Fatima week is in its third day." She said that *now* we must respond *urgently* to the basic requests of Fatima and with *many* more First Saturday Communions of Reparation.

This "third day," which we will explain further in another chapter, refers to a phase of the time heading to the triumph. We can safely speak of times which have passed and times into which we are entering without, as Cardinal Sodano said, specific dates.

The last part of the Fatima Secret, more fully explained at Akita, might be *the last sign* for our times before chastisement—the *final* call to do what is necessary to mitigate or to avoid it.

The revelation of the first part of the Fatima Secret, as we suggested in the first chapter, was delayed for at least two major reasons:

1) So as not to interfere with the investigation of the supernatural character of the apparition, and;

2) At the time of the apparition (1917), it would have been difficult to understand.

Why in Japan?

There are similar reasons why the third part, describing the vision of the Angel with the flaming sword to set fire to the earth, was not revealed until 2000, and why it was first revealed in Japan.

In 1917, Our Lady had said: "Men must stop offending God, Who is so much offended." Yet, despite the Great Miracle "that all may believe," men not only continued to offend God but there followed a *worldwide collapse of morality* in the aftermath of seventy years of atheism spread from Russia throughout the world—seventy years of ignoring the Fatima message.

The Role of the Atomic Bomb

Our Lady chose to give the reminder of possible "annihilation of nations" in Japan where the first (and until 2000, the only) atomic bombs were used to wipe out entire cities in a single flash.

Now atomic bombs stocked in different parts of the world are *more than enough to wipe out "a great part of humanity."* Urgency grows since the dissolution of the Soviet Union, because *control and containment of many of those bombs is being lost.*

When asked: "What is the message of Akita?" the Bishop answered simply: "*It is the message of Fatima.*"

The Bishop knew then, from *the actual custodian* in Rome *of the Third Secret* of Fatima, that this was consistent with the REST of the message of Fatima. It was the reminder of the prophecy of "annihilation of nations" made in 1917 which now, in this atomic age, was (in the very words of Our Lady at Akita) at hand.

It is meaningful, too, that the message given in Akita was first revealed in March of 1984, just after the Pope, in union with all the bishops of the world, had finally fulfilled one of the basic requests of Fatima: *The Collegial Consecration to the Immaculate Heart.*

"Several Entire Nations Will Be Annihilated"

Despite the many miracles that confirmed the Akita message, and despite the careful and prudent investigation by ecclesiastical authority, will those who did not accept it do so now after the release of the Third Secret?

In an article published in *Voice of the Sacred Hearts* in 1993, Bishop Ito (the Bishop of Akita) wrote:

> "Traveling to Rome in 1988, I conferred with Cardinal Ratzinger, the Prefect of the Congregation for the Doctrine of the Faith. Voicing no objections to the overall content of my pastoral letter, he did, however, recommend that the Japan Conference of Bishops assemble a committee to investigate it in detail. This meeting took place November 29, 1990, with all the members of the standing committee in attendance.
>
> "While we discussed the phenomena of Akita, Archbishop Shirayanagi of Tokyo, who is chairman of the Bishops' Conference, read a letter from Bishop Francisco Keiichi Sato, the acting Bishop of Akita (Niigata).

"Bishop Sato, who accepted my pastoral letter, remarked that there are numerous pilgrimages to the site in Akita and that conversions and miraculous cures have taken place there.

"Based upon such evidence, neither Bishop Sato nor the members of the standing committee thought it necessary to undertake further investigation."

Despite all this, the message of Akita was ignored even after publication of Father Yasuda's book[20] with approval of the Bishop.

We presume that it was because of so much widespread reluctance to accept so severe a message that *Cardinal Ratzinger suggested to the Bishop of Akita that there be a public acknowledgment of the authenticity of the Akita events by the Japanese episcopate. This appeared in 1996 in Japan's national Catholic press.*

Too Late?

It is sad to know that it is too late for hundreds of thousands who were warned by Our Lady in Rwanda and the Balkans, but even sadder to think that unless we awaken to our responsibility to do as Our Lady asks, it will be too late for "*a great part of humanity.*"

One of the visionaries in Rwanda was heard to say to Our Lady: "I know what makes you sad. It is because your message will not be heard until it is too late."

We hear a similar message from many other sources. In *Divine Inspirations,*[21] we read:

---

[20] *AKITA, The Tears and Message of Mary,* by Teiji Yasuda, OSV, translated by John M. Haffert. Published by the 101 Foundation in 1989, 202 pp.

"The world is now approaching its terrifying purification...*the greatest chastisement since the world began.*"

And in other parts:

"*You are ever closer to the chastisement* (written in 1996). Wake up from your slumber. Stay awake! Pray to be able to withstand these terrible times... The chastisement can be lessened by prayer. Pray for deliverance... A chastisement the like of which has never been, or ever will be again. Shout it from the rooftops. Do not be afraid of anyone. Go and proclaim this message. Prepare now! Atone, suffer, pray, prepare."

The message is not to frighten but to show us the alternative and to move us to respond. St. Thomas Aquinas says God threatens punishment so we will avoid it. We must face the alternative to our continued complacency and failure to respond to all these urgent messages from Heaven. And Pope John Paul II said the importance of Fatima is that Our Lady has indicated *the specific response* needed to **"save mankind from self-destruction."**

That is not a call to fear but to hope! Our Lady has given us *the specific response needed to purify the world by Grace rather than by fire.*

This message, which has at its core an Act of Consecration to the Immaculate Heart of Mary, must spread.

Yet blocking the spread of the message is not only reluctance to speak of mankind's self-destruc-

---

[21] This book of messages from Jesus and Mary, first published in Slovakia with Imprimatur of Archdiocese of Prague in 1996, was published in 1999 by Queenship Publishing Co., Goletea, CA 93116. It includes an introductory letter by Most Rev. Bishop G. F. Mayne, D.D.

tion as the alternative to our failed response but, as we have said, also because of *a failure to understand an essential element of that response: Consecration to the Immaculate Heart of Mary.*

Photo of the miraculous image of Our Lady of Akita as seen on the cover of the book *Akita—The Tears and Message of Mary* by Father Yasuda, translated into English by John M. Haffert and published by the 101 Foundation, the name of which is based on the 101 times the statue shed tears.

CHAPTER 5

The Last Marian Dogma

Needed for the Triumph.

A S WE SAID in the first chapter, the heart of the response asked at Fatima is to establish in the world devotion to the Immaculate Heart of Mary.

A very important statement in the Vatican document on the Third Secret seems to have been completely ignored. It states:

> "It might be objected that we should not place a human being between ourselves and Christ. But then we remember that Paul did not hesitate to say to his communities: 'Imitate me' (1 Cor 4:16; Phil 3;17;1 Th 1:6, and 3:7, 9). *In the Apostle, they could see concretely what it meant to follow Christ. But from whom might we better learn in every age than from the Mother of the Lord?*"

A challenge of the revealed Secret, not at first apparent to many, *involves the intermediary role of Mary.*

On May 14, 2000, this writer was privileged to spend three hours with two internationally recognized authorities who had attended the ceremonies of the beatification of Francisco and Jacinta the day before: Dr. Mark Miravalle of *Vox Populi*, and Howard Dee, former Ambassador to the Holy See and author of *Mankind's Final Destiny.*

Together, we had heard the startling news about the release of the Third Secret.

Ambassador Dee had been told in person by the Most Rev. John Ito, Bishop of Akita, that Cardinal Ratzinger had reassured His Excellency about publication of the message of Akita on the grounds that it was similar to the Third Secret of Fatima. Separately, Bishop Ito had told this also to myself.

Although Ambassador Dee was sure he had not misunderstood Bishop Ito, *he personally asked Cardinal Ratzinger if indeed the message of Akita was essentially the message of the Third Secret.*

The Cardinal affirmed that it was.

Would Such a Message Be Made Public?

At Akita, Our Lady spoke of *fire* devastating much of the world in a *"chastisement worse than the Deluge,"* which "so far," She has been able to hold back.

All three of us, who had just learned that the Secret would now be revealed, wondered how the world would react to such a message. Even within the Church, the Fatima message has often been belittled. And with so much skepticism in the world, what would be the reaction to an announcement of a chastisement "worse than the Deluge" if men continued to ignore God?

The Pope was making a daring initiative. He apparently saw the Great Jubilee as the time to take radical action to awaken the world to the Fatima message. But he gave time for the Congregation for the Doctrine of the Faith to explain it.

The Secret, with the explanation, came six weeks later. Its connection with the more complete message of Akita was the vision of the Angel of Justice about to set fire to the earth but prevented by Our Lady. Obviously, the Secret was not for the world, which would scoff at it. It was for the Church, which had to act upon it.

Is this not why Cardinal Ratzinger, even before the directive of the Pope, had seen fit to make known that the message given by Our Lady at Akita was consonant with the Third Secret? It would also explain why the Cardinal, to remove all doubts about the supernaturalism of the apparitions of Akita, urged that they be ratified by the Japanese Episcopal Conference.

This shows again that there was no intention of keeping the Secret from those within the Church who can act upon it. There was only concern that it be done prudently.

Time for the Marian Dogma

We felt greatly encouraged by the May 13th announcement about the Third Secret. Pope John Paul II was, in a sense, taking things into his own hands.

Dr. Miravalle had been leading an international effort for an understanding of the need to define that Mary is Co-Redemptrix, Mediatrix, and Advocate. Like the Third Secret, might this new dogma be too great a shock to the world in general—the secularist world of the new millennium?

There is no question that the Church itself is ready. That Mary is Co-Redemptrix, Mediatrix, and Advocate has been for centuries proclaimed by doctors and saints as a part of Catholic belief.

But how can we speak to the world about it? How can we present the mystery of Mary's mediation to a doubting, often scoffing world? What can we do about those who seek even within the Church, if only for reasons of ecumenism, to downplay Marian devotion and to ignore Her role in the economy of salvation?

Role of the Immaculate Heart

We were not told at Fatima that God wishes to establish devotion to the Immaculate Heart just among Catholics. The words were: "God wishes to establish *in the world* devotion to the Immaculate Heart of Mary." What is that devotion? How will we inculcate it in Catholics? in Protestants? in the world?

Monsignor Ronald Knox, convert son of the Anglican Bishop of Manchester and great Oxford scholar, said in his book *The Belief of Catholics*:

> "They have said that we Catholics deify Her. That is not because we exaggerate the eminence of God's Mother, but because they belittle the eminence of God. A creature miraculously preserved from sin by the indwelling power of the Holy Spirit, that is to them a divine title... They refuse to honor the God-bearing Woman because their Christ is only a God-bearing man."

On January 12, 2000, in one of the first audiences of the Jubilee Year, Pope John Paul II said:

"God willed Mary's presence in the history of salvation. When He decided to send His Son into the world, He willed that He should come to us by being born of a woman (Cf. Gal 4.4).

"Therefore Mary is on the road that goes *from the Father to humanity* as the Mother who gives everyone Her Savior Son. At the same time, She is on the road that men must take to go *to the Father through Christ in the Spirit* (Cf. Eph. 2,18).

"Consequently, as the Council emphasized in *Lumen Gentium* (N. 60): "Mary's function as mother of men in no way obscures or diminishes this unique mediation of Christ, but rather shows its power."

"As I said expressly in the encyclical *Redemptoris Mater*, Mary's maternal mediation "is the mediation of Christ" (N. 38).[22]

Only when Mary is understood can Christ, as God-Man, be understood. Only when we understand the action of the Holy Spirit in Mary, for the God-Man's incarnation, can we understand His personal relation to each of us.[23]

The triumph of the Sacred Heart will come only with the triumph of the Immaculate Heart of His Mother. The triumph of the Holy Spirit will come only with the triumph of His spouse, the Mother of Jesus. When She said, "My Immaculate Heart will triumph," She was speaking of the triumph of Her Son and of Her Spouse.

---

[22] *Inside the Vatican*, February 2000, pg. 74. The editor commented that the Pope's words could mean "that even serious objections to the dogma can be answered if one explains Mary's mediating role in the correct way."

[23] This thought deserves deep reflection. It relates to the "new and divine holiness" to which we refer from time to time throughout these pages.

St. Grignion de Montfort said it over three hundred years ago:

"Up to this time Mary has been unknown. That is why Jesus Christ is not known as He ought to be. If the knowledge and the Kingdom of Jesus Christ are to come into the world they will be *the necessary consequence* of the knowledge and kingdom (triumph) of the most holy Mary who brought Him into the world the first time, and will make His second advent full of splendor."[24]

That is why the fifth Marian dogma is necessary. It is the solemn definition of *the truth of Mary's role in redemption as the new Eve, and the truth that Her "Yes" to the Angel at Nazareth is still operative in the flow of Grace to the world.* Nothing less dramatic than making this a dogma might sufficiently focus the world's attention upon it and make it understood.

Can we think of any more effective way to wake up the world to the truth?

The Primacy of Jesus

How else will the world come to understand the real meaning of consecration to the Immaculate Heart of Mary, and of the great value of total consecration to this Immaculate Heart as the quickest and surest way to great sanctity?

This consecration is called by St. Grignion de Montfort "true" devotion to Mary because Jesus is its goal. Any devotion not related to Jesus is false. The saint says:

---

[24] *True Devotion to the Blessed Virgin*, 12-38.

"Jesus Christ our Savior, true God and true Man, ought to be the last end of all our devotions, else they are false and delusive.

"Jesus Christ is the Alpha and the Omega, the beginning and the end, of all things. We labor not, as the Apostle says, except to render every man perfect in Jesus Christ, because it is in Him alone that the whole plenitude of the Divinity dwells... He is our only Master...our only Head to Whom we must be united, our only Model to Whom we should conform ourselves, our only Physician Who can heal us, our one Shepherd Who can feed us, our only Truth Whom we must believe, our only Life Who can animate us, our only ALL in all things Who can satisfy us.

"*There has been no other name given under Heaven, except the name of Jesus by which we can be saved.* God has laid no other foundation of our salvation, our perfection, or our glory, than Jesus Christ. Every building which is not built on that firm rock is founded upon the moving sand, and sooner or later infallibly will fall.

"By Jesus Christ, with Jesus Christ, in Jesus Christ, we can do all things; we can render all honor and glory to the Father in the unity of the Holy Spirit; we can become perfect ourselves..."[25]

It is only after saying this that St. Grignion adds that "Devotion to Mary is *necessary for us as a means of finding Jesus perfectly,* of loving Him tenderly, of serving Him faithfully."[26]

---

[25] *True Devotion to the Blessed Virgin*, nos. 61, 62.
[26] Ibid.

Mother of God Dogma

It was difficult, even under threats of schism, for the Council of Ephesus to define that Mary is Mother of GOD. But only by that definition could the world know beyond doubt that Her Son is both man *and* GOD. It was not so much to honor Mary that the *Mother of God* dogma was proclaimed. It was to defend *the dual nature of Christ in one Divine Person.*

With modern science it is easier to understand, and therefore easier to believe, that Mary is Mother of God. The DNA of a mother's appendix is the same as in every other part of her body. But the DNA of a child in her womb, *from the moment of conception,* is entirely different from that of her own body. *It is another person.* And in the womb of Mary, *that other Person,* conceived there by the Holy Spirit, *is a Divine Person who has assumed a second nature, the nature of man.*[27]

How wonderful that millions have believed this for sixteen hundred years just on simple faith. They have believed without clarification of modern science and the testimony of the doctor-saints of all those centuries.

Not Primarily to Honor Mary

The fifth Marian dogma is not primarily to honor Mary but to confirm the Merciful plan of God *raising us to Him* through co-redemption, mediation, and advocacy.

---

[27] This has special meaning today in relation to abortion. The "pro-choice" woman can decide to have an appendix cut out because it is part of her body, but she cannot choose to have a fetus cut out because it is not part of her body. From the moment of conception, it is another person.

The Church has always believed this truth. It has been affirmed over and over throughout the ages with less controversy than the Divine Maternity and the Immaculate Conception, both of which were finally affirmed dogmatically.

But now we have to deal with a divided Christianity. And we have to deal with an increasing diminution of faith and devotion within the Church. A priest who was recently asked (March 2000) why he chose to become a priest, answered:

"Perhaps you should ask why I *remain* a priest since sixteen were ordained in my class and only two remain. *I have retained my devotion to Mary.*"

We are asked to establish in the world devotion to the Immaculate Heart of Mary at a time when Her advocacy is so needed, yet when Her devotion has diminished within the Church and is considered idolatry by some Christians outside the Church.

The dogma can lead to the necessary explanation. It can, in a sense, *force* the explanation of Our Lady's mediating role.

Of course, objections are raised. Can we not expect Satan to see to that? Our Lady has promised that when the dogma is proclaimed, the triumph will begin. We will finally have obeyed the Will of God Who wishes "to establish in the world devotion to the Immaculate Heart of Mary."

We say again, it is not because Our Lady said so—it is because *when the dogma is proclaimed, the role of Mary in God's plan for our salvation will be explained.*

As when the Church in 431 proclaimed Her Mother of God, and in 1854 defined Her Immaculate Conception (followed by the apparitions at Lourdes), the sky will not fall in. Rather the clouds of doubts and obscurities will pass and the sun of a beautiful truth will shine.

We will acknowledge that God chose to become MAN, through a real human being, a real woman, who by that fact became the new Eve, the new mother of us all in the order of Grace. We will acknowledge that we *owe everything to Her* because She said, "Yes."

That "Yes" remains operative at every moment. That is why we call her "Mediatrix" even though, between God and man, Jesus is the sole Mediator. *Her mediation is the consent that brought the Mediator into the world and to the Cross*, as was affirmed by the Second Vatican Council:

> "The motherhood of Mary in the order of Grace continues uninterruptedly from the consent which She loyally gave at the Annunciation and which She sustained without wavering beneath the cross, until the eternal fulfillment of all the elect. Taken up to Heaven, She did not lay aside this saving office... Therefore, the Blessed Virgin is invoked in the Church under the titles of Advocate, Helper, Benefactress, and Mediatrix..." (LG 62:969).

For Our Separated Brethren

There are many Protestant evangelists today who preach the doctrine of the Trinity and of the Divinity of Jesus. They are reaching millions by television all over the world.

As we listen to their affirmation of Jesus as "the Way, the Truth, the Life," we recall His own words in Luke 9, 49: "Do not prevent him, for whoever is not against you is for you." And in Mark 10, 38:

"There is no one who performs a mighty work in My name who can at the same time speak ill of Me."

Are we not doing Protestants an injustice to presume they will not understand something as simple as the continuing operation of Mary's "Yes" to the Incarnation and to Calvary? Catholics have believed it for centuries. But how can we expect it to be adequately explained to others *until we explain it definitively to ourselves?*

Because they are not instructed in what we really believe about Mary does not mean that our separated brethren are *incapable* of knowing and understanding.

On my first trip to Europe by air in 1946, I happened to be sitting behind Dr. Ralph Sockman who at the time was the most celebrated Protestant pastor on national radio. I used to listen to him every Sunday. When the plane landed to refuel at Gander (crossing the Atlantic in those days took 19 hours), I told him so. He walked with me on the airport tarmac for almost an hour.

I told him that in all the many times I heard him preach, I never heard him say one thing that I, as a Catholic, did not believe.

"There was one time," he said, "when I spoke of the brothers of Jesus." Then he said: "But is it not true that you Catholics deify Mary?"

I explained what we understood by the title "Mother of God" (as I did above). We became friends. When I wrote my book on the Eucharist, his review was one of the most flattering. And when I invited him to come on television with me later to speak about the Eucharist, he accepted to the amazement of many because he had turned down many other invitations.

He understood what we believed *at once* when it was explained with sincere faith, because he was himself a man of faith.

And so we should presume are MOST of our separated brethren.

Another Example

On October 7, 1961, among the eight thousand pilgrims and town leaders who welcomed the Pilgrim Virgin Statue in Weingarten, Germany, was the Reverend Mr. Baumann, a much-esteemed Protestant clergyman. Addressing the crowd in the presence of the famous Fatima image traveling towards Russia, he said:

> "We pray with our Catholic brethren that the peace of Christ may reign throughout the entire world... We are with Mary at the foot of the Cross of Christ, disposing ourselves to receive peace, a Grace, which comes to us from the Cross... We are suddenly aware that Mary is Mother of God. We have some one hundred and thirty sermons of Luther on the most holy Virgin Mary in which he sings of all her glorious privileges subsequently rejected by the majority of Protestants.
>
> "It is permitted also to us Protestants to rejoice with Mary. Let us unite with all the Church in our thirst for peace. When we see our Catholic brethren presenting to the world the message of Fatima, we heartily thank them for their yes to the Mother of God."[27]

This is a big, a VERY big loose end from our past century—and beyond.

---

[27] *Ce Que La Vierge Nous Demande*, by Canon Barthas, pg. 205.

Now Is the Time

Our first obligation is to pray with loving confidence to overcome efforts of Satan to confuse and to prevent this definition. *The fifth Marian dogma will be necessary for the unity of the Church.* It is feared by Satan as he fears little else. Yet *now is the time.*

Our Lady of All Nations said: "With passing years, apostasy and unbelief will set in. The Lady of All Nations stands here (as Co-Redemptrix, Mediatrix, and Advocate) and says I want to help them, and I am allowed to help them... It is time to unite."

Thinking I might be writing my last book in 1997 (*The Day I Didn't Die*), I dedicated several pages to this subject (almost all of chapters 7, 10, 16 and 17). I mentioned then, as I have in the last chapter, the great importance of the declarations of the Vicar of Christ, especially in the encyclicals.

Our Lady of All Nations, speaking of the importance of encyclicals, said: "*Do you realize how powerful is this force? Know well that your time has come.* The Father and the Son now send the Co-Redemptrix, Mediatrix and Advocate over the whole world. *They both wish to send the Holy Spirit Who alone can bring peace.*"

The dogma "Mother of God" affirmed the dual nature of Jesus in one Divine Person. The new Marian dogma will affirm the role of the Holy Spirit.

Two thousand years ago, God chose to *establish a relationship* with the humble maid of Nazareth, the relationship of *mother* through the mystery of His Incarnation. At the same time, He established a special relationship with His Third Person, the Holy Spirit—*the relationship of co-operator.*

It is About the Holy Spirit

This was impressed upon me in an extraordinary manner. It was like passing a hill of rubbish about a hundred feet in diameter and fifty feet high and hearing a voice inside you say, "In that vast pile, there is a diamond. Walk fifty-two feet to the right, around the pile, then dig in 18 inches above the ground and reach in. It will be there."

In May of 1996, I entered a huge library in Rome to select a book. Without hesitation, I walked past stacks of hundreds upon hundreds of books, turned a corner, reached up to a middle shelf where my hand, as though guided by a mind other than my own, took hold of a "diamond" which contained a message which subsequently proved of great value to the cause of the dogma.[28]

The author of the book was Luis Cardinal Menendez, previously unknown to me. I learned later that he is an internationally respected theologian whose cause for canonization is under way. The Cardinal wrote:

"Two sanctifiers are necessary to souls—the Holy Spirit and the Virgin Mary. For They are the only ones Who can reproduce Christ.

"The first is the Sanctifier *by essence* because He is God, Infinite Sanctity—and it belongs to Him to communicate to souls the mystery of that sanctity.

"The Virgin Mary for Her part is *the co-operator*, the indispensable instrument, in and by God's design.

"These two, then, the Holy Spirit and Mary, are the indispensable artificers of Jesus, the

---

[28] For the full story, see chapter 16 of *The Day I Didn't Die*, published by the 101 Foundation.

indispensable sanctifiers of souls.

"Saints in Heaven can co-operate in the sanctification of souls, but their co-operation is not necessary—while the co-operation of these two Artisans of Jesus is so necessary that without it, souls are not sanctified (and this is by actual design of Providence).

"The Virgin Mary has the efficacious influence of Mediatrix in the most profound and delicate operation of Grace in our souls.

"Such is the place that the Holy Spirit and the Virgin Mary have in the order of sanctification. Therefore, Christian piety should put

Image of Our Lady of All Nations of which the cult and prayer were approved on May 31, 1996. A wood sculpture of this image "came alive" at Akita on October 13, 1973 to deliver a startling message to the world, which Cardinal Ratzinger said was consonant with the last Secret of Fatima.

these two Artisans of Christ in their true place, *making devotion to them something necessary, profound, and constant. The Sanctifier by His Essence...the Virgin Mary the Co-Operator, the indispensable instrument.*"

In asking for this dogma, Our Lady instructed us to pray:

"Lord Jesus Christ, send now Your Holy Spirit over the earth! Let the Holy Spirit reign in the hearts of all peoples to save them from corruption, disaster, and war. May the Lady of All Nations, who once was Mary, be our advocate."

As we said above, the dogma "Mother of God" affirmed the intervention of the Second Person of the Trinity into our world as truly man born of Mary, and the new dogma is to affirm the intervention of the Third Person of the Trinity into our world as the Spouse of Mary, the new Eve.

This dogma is an affirmation of God's Will that the Holy Spirit be sent NOW over all the earth to "live in the hearts of ALL," as He lived in the heart of Mary when she said: "Be it done to me according to your word."[29]

---

[29] We are told that "Rome" asked that no more petitions be sent to the Vatican. However, it is traditional to gather such petitions. Specifically in reference to this new dogma, the Holy Father himself has spoken of the importance of the *vox populi*. The petitions, even if they served no other purpose, are *prayers* for the solemn affirmation of what Catholics have long believed about the place of Mary in the economy of salvation, and they are prayers that this sublime doctrine will be understood. To aid directly in promotion of the dogma, contact *Vox Populi*. See the author's books *NOW The Woman Shall Conquer* and *The Day I Didn't Die*.

God Wills It

Many felt that current attitudes in the Church at the turn of the millennium made proclamation of the dogma virtually impossible. But nothing is impossible with God.

"God wishes to establish in the world devotion to the Immaculate Heart of Mary." God wills that ALL the world knows that it has a Mother given twice: First when an Angel asked if She would be the Mother of our Redeemer, and again when the Redeemer said from the Cross: "Behold your Mother."

As He came to the world through Her 2,000 years ago, so now He wills to come in a new way—a way most of us cannot yet even begin to grasp. *It will be the new era of divine holiness. It will be a time of Grace such as the world will not have known since man was expelled from Eden.*

What Can We Do?

As said above, what we must do first and foremost is pray—preferably with fasting or some other form of sacrifice. This is not a matter of reasoning and argument. It is a spiritual matter. It is at the very crux of spiritual warfare.

Second, we ourselves can seek to understand better why we believe that Our Lady was chosen by God not only to be associated with Him as Mother but also associated with Him in undoing the sin of Eve, in being indeed the NEW Eve, joining with Him in restoring man to God.

The better we understand, the better we can help explain to others.

Holy Advice

Readers of my most recent books may know that I have a sister in the Carmelite Order who prays and suffers. She entered Carmel when I wrote my first book some sixty years before I wrote this one. Over the years, whenever there was a victory in the apostolate, she had to suffer. And in 1996, when I wrote the book *The Day I Didn't Die*, was it Satan, or just an accident, which flung her down an iron staircase almost causing her death?

When I sent her the initial "notes" of this present book, she had one comment:

"Perhaps now is the time to promote what is most theological about our Blessed Virgin. We cannot esteem Her or love Her too much: *Mother of God and Mother of the human fam-*

Sister Therese of the Queen of Carmel, D.C., sister of the author, who gave up the world in a Carmelite cloister and became the spiritual support of his apostolate.

ily. What more can be said? What limits can there be to our hope? The words taught to us to be said at the end of each decade of the Rosary ('O My Jesus, forgive us our sins, save us from the fires of Hell, lead all souls to Heaven and help especially those most in need') is like a translation of 'Thy Kingdom come, Thy will be done on earth as it is in Heaven.'"

Based on Solid Doctrine

With solid doctrine comes solid devotion. Understanding the teaching of the Church about Mary results in ever-greater love.

We find solid doctrine in the papal encyclicals, which constantly update our understanding of what God has taught us through Scripture, tradition, and the doctors of the Church.

Dr. Miravalle, founder of *Vox Populi*, meets with Pope John Paul II.

We cannot wait for the Mediatrix dogma to make this known.

There are at least three papal encyclicals of special relevance to the message of Fatima, to the Secret of Fatima, and indeed, to almost all that we are saying in this book. They are: **The Great Sign** (*Signum Magnum*), by Pope Paul VI; **To The Queen of the World** (*Ad Caeli Reginam*) by Pope Pius XII; and **Mother of the Redeemer** (*Redemptoris Mater*) by Pope John Paul II.

A "popular" explanation of the first two of these encyclicals will be found in the author's book *NOW the Woman Shall Conquer.*

In *Mother of the Redeemer*, the Pope recommends the *totus tuus* devotion of St. Grignion de Montfort, which is of special importance in meeting the challenge to the new century.

If we begin seriously to develop true devotion to Mary, based on the solid teaching of the encyclicals, we will begin to long to hear Jesus say to us what He said to Saint John Eudes: "I have given you this admirable Heart of My dearest Mother to be *one with yours* so that you might have a heart worthy of Mine."

Satan does his best to obscure doctrine. But the Queen of the World reveals it.

Satan has his servants. The Woman, destined in Scripture to crush his head, also has Hers.

We know *who* will win. *When* depends on us. Will it be after annihilation of some entire nations, or will it be before so that, by doing what Our Lady asks, the chastisement may be avoided?

CHAPTER 6

The Third Day

"Fatima is in the Third Day. The triumph is an ongoing process." –Sister Lucia
It is the time for spiritual awareness.

URING AN INTERVIEW with Cardinal Vidal on October 11, 1993, the visionary of Fatima said that we are in the "third day," in which the triumph is an "ongoing process."

For millions, *it is as though this third day never dawned.* Millions seem either not to know, or not to realize, that with repeated Divine interventions, *God is making a "final effort,"* as Saint Margaret Mary said, *to awaken the conscience of the world.*

To the average person it seems as if these signs from Heaven were not even happening. Economic well being and hedonism seem to blind men and women to the Fatima message. Others seem to think a message given in 1917 is no longer urgent. Sister Lucia told the Cardinal:

> "All the wars which have occurred could have been avoided through prayer and sacrifice. This is the reason Our Lady asked for the Communion

of Reparation (on First Saturdays) and the consecration.

"People expect things to happen immediately within their own time frame. But Fatima is still in its third day. *The triumph is an ongoing process.*"

Then, repeating herself, she said:

"Fatima is still in its third day. We are now in the post consecration period... *Fatima has just begun.* How can one expect it to be over immediately?"

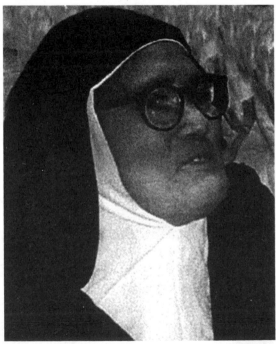

Sister Lucia as the author saw her on May 31, 1999, the day of the Golden Jubilee of her profession as a Carmelite nun. The author had just published his book *Too Late?* based on the startling messages given by Sister Lucia in October, 1993, in which she said an atomic war had been avoided in 1985, and that we are now in the "third day of the Fatima week."

Just For Catholics?

After saying a second time that "Fatima has just begun," Sister Lucia added:

> "The Rosary, which is the most important spiritual weapon we have in these times when the devil is so active, should be recited."

Asked about the Apostolate (with the pledge and the emphasis on First Saturdays) and devotion to the Sacred Hearts, she said:

> "This movement shows itself to be the fulfillment of what the Virgin asked. *To promote the Communion of Reparation is the means to combat atheism...* The Virgin is interested in everything (the entire pledge) but particularly in the Communions of Reparation."

The author, left, with John Marto, brother of Blessed Francisco and Jacinta. Known by the author for more than fifty years, he died only three days before May 13th when the Pope beatified his brother and sister.

In this "third day" following the change in Russia, *the progress of the ongoing triumph will depend on how many respond to the basic requests of Fatima,* the first of which was given on the day of the miracle: *"Men must stop offending God* Who is already so much offended."

This does not exclude our Protestant brethren. Jesus said: "Whoever is not against us is for us" (Mark 10,38). A Protestant televangelist like John Hagee may mistakenly think Catholics adore statues, but he thunders against abortion and sodomy and injustice, and he preaches Jesus as the Way, the Truth, and the Life. He must be very dear to the Heavenly Mother he doesn't know.

We praise and bless God for all the wonderful Protestant evangelists who are apostles of Jesus today like the unnamed man in the gospel who preached and worked miracles in the name of Jesus. When the apostles complained: "He does not follow in our company," Jesus said that he was nevertheless "for" us (Luke 9, 49).

In this third day, when we expect a great triumph of Grace in the world, the Holy Spirit is intervening not only with messages from Our Lady but also *directly to many hearts.* It is primarily Catholics who sin against the Eucharist, which St. Thomas Aquinas said is one of the gravest of all sins. And Catholics, with the continuity of the faith from Jesus, have the primary obligation to make Communions of Reparation. They have a *special* responsibility, as did the Jews who had the continuity of faith from Abraham and Moses when Jesus came.

What Is the Third Day?

Sister Lucia, who was left on earth to follow through with the entire Fatima message, *had carefully prepared her statement to the Cardinal about the third day.*[30]

This impressed me so much that I first titled my second-last book THE THIRD DAY.[31] I had considered over and over what the expression "the third day" might mean.

At first, I could not find a satisfactory answer.

Then a reference, given by Biblical scholar Abbot Delisi,[32] to a passage in the book *Poem of the Man-God* (of which we shall speak later) led me to the prophecy of Hosea:

"He will revive us after two days. *On the third day, He will raise us up to live in His Presence.*

"Let us know, let us strive to know the Lord, as certain as the dawn is His coming, and His judgment shines forth like the light of day."[33]

Also, we recall the prophecy of Daniel, chapter 12:

"Blessed is the man who has patience and perseveres...*you shall rise for your reward at the end of the days.*"

---

[30] Sister Lucia had conversed with the Cardinal in Spanish, a language well known to her because she had spent over twenty-five years in Spain. But this statement on the third day she made in Portuguese, breaking off the interview with the Cardinal to speak through an interpreter. It was obviously a statement she had carefully prepared and wanted to give *exactly*. We must think that it was inspired, or perhaps even given, by Our Lady.

[31] The final title of the book is *Too Late?*. For its importance, see footnote above.

[32] Most Rev. Anthony Delisi, O.C.S.O, prepared over 1,600 scriptural references to the *Poem*, page by page for all five volumes. Available from Holy Spirit Monastery, Conyers, GA.

[33] Hosea, VI, 2.

The passage in the *Poem*, which recalled these scriptures, describes the meeting of Our Lord with the apostles three days before the great Passover celebration and the beginning of His Passion. He says:

> "Bear in mind that these are the words of the prophet: *After two days...that is two periods of eternity...the third day will come...*we shall rise in His Presence in the Kingdom of Christ on the Earth and we *shall live before Him in the triumph of the spirit.*"[34]

Could this mean that the "third day" after the redemption, the beginning of the third millennium, will be the day of "His Presence in the Kingdom of Christ on the Earth—the era of living before Him in the triumph of the spirit?"

This might be the deeper meaning of Sister Lucia's words: *"We are living now in the third day...the triumph is an ongoing process."*

Time for Spiritual Awareness

We must be aware of the possibility (and some would say, probability) of a chastisement. We must make sinners aware that a chastisement "worse than the Deluge" is the alternative to continuation in evil.

But while conscious of the alternative, we focus in hope on the special Graces now flowing in this time of Mercy. May we not expect to see *wonders of Grace*, eminently including Christian unity?

In four books, one after the other from 1997 to 2000, this author has felt impelled to say that *the triumph has already begun*. Those who respond positively to the great event (the illumination of conscience) are about to experience, in light from the

---

[34] *Poem of the Man-God*, Vol. V, pg. 424.

Immaculate Heart of Mary, *spiritual awareness* that can change the face of the earth.

We had a preview of this in the first apparition of Fatima when, in the light from Mary's Heart, the children *felt "lost in God,"* and cried out, "O Most Holy Trinity, I adore Thee! My God, My God, I love Thee in the Most Blessed Sacrament."

That awareness is available now.

Catholics have the special advantage of the Scapular and the Rosary, the signs of Our Lady's Heart and of Her mysteries. With Her Sign over our hearts and the touch of Her Rosary, *we can be aware* that Our Lady is listening, loving, and leading us to Jesus. She in turn will make us aware of *His Physical Presence in the Eucharist and of His Spiritual Presence at every moment.* She will inspire us to say the words She taught the children of Fatima *with every act of the day*:

"O My Jesus! It is for love of You! In reparation for the offenses committed against the Immaculate Heart of Mary![35] And for the conversion of poor sinners!"

This is the time of Mercy! This is the time to anticipate the gift of living in the Divine Will! This is the time of the answer to two millenniums of the prayer: *"Thy Will be done on earth as it is in Heaven."* This is the dawn of the day of Divine awareness.

Awareness of God

Even many devout persons who pray rarely get "through" to supernatural awareness. Words, sincerely meant, can be said without the person saying them being fully *aware* that *God is listening.*

---

[35] Abortion, sins of impurity, sacrilegious and careless Communions.

But for those who persevere in saying the words sincerely, there comes a moment of light, a moment of awareness of the supernatural. It is a wonderful Divine experience, transitory for some but transforming for others.

We are challenged to look through the exteriors of life to the real world beneath them. St. Faustina exclaimed: "Oh, how beautiful is the world of the spirit! And *so real* that, by comparison, the exterior life is *just a vain illusion...*"

To gaze *through* the exteriors of life to the real world beneath is like looking at a flat stereogram and suddenly, yet almost imperceptibly, finding oneself looking "through" the flat picture into the depths of three dimensions.

Spiritually it is like looking through all the circumstances and realities around us and suddenly seeing the greater reality—the reality of God. And it is breathtaking. As Saint Faustina said: "By comparison, the exterior life is just a vain illusion."

Oh, how we would wish that mere words or comparisons could give this vision, this awareness. And how sad that many good persons go through their entire lives without experiencing it!

Now is the time of Grace. It is the third day in which "the triumph is an ongoing process." It is the time of Mercy, *the time to see through natural and transitory realities to the greater reality of the supernatural world.* We would wish for a magic formula, as simple as gazing "through" a stereogram.

This is what Our Lady gave us at Fatima.

The "Magic" Formula

In 1946, Sister Lucia, who was left in this world to show how the promise of triumph could be obtained, formulated the requests of Our Lady into a "pledge." It is the "magic" formula.

It consists of extending our Morning Offering through the day, sanctifying ordinary daily duties in reparation for our sins and the sins of the world. It offers two aids: the sign of consecration to Her Heart—the Scapular, and the door to the mysteries of Her Heart—the Rosary. It is the magic formula that opens to us the most pure Heart of Mary.

Added to this formula is the urgent post-request of Our Lady for Communions of Reparation on the First Saturday of each month. The four conditions are the Rosary, fifteen minutes of meditation on the mysteries of the Rosary, Confession, and Communion—all offered in reparation for the sins committed against the Immaculate Heart of Mary on five consecutive First Saturdays.

Confession is required whether or not one is in mortal sin. It is reparation for those who do not go to confession, and it is preparation for a worthy Communion of Reparation.

At Pellevoisin, Our Lady said that what MOST offends Her Immaculate Heart is "careless Communions." And She asks for Communions of Reparation.

Purity of Heart

Jesus named eight beatitudes. It was *purity of heart* which bore His promise: *"They shall see God."*

Devotion to the Immaculate Heart of Mary is at the heart of the magic formula because Her Heart is not only a model but also an intercessory aid to purity.

Often throughout these pages, we make reference to the "new and divine holiness," which will prevail in the time of the triumph. We speak of the *totus tuus* consecration as the "elevator" to this degree of holiness. The first step is the Fatima pledge.

One of the greatest rewards to that pledge, as we say elsewhere in these pages, is the Sabbatine Privilege, which offers the hope that we shall be "freed from Purgatory by the first Saturday after death."

In addition to the basic Fatima pledge, *the only other requirement for this privilege is chastity according to one's state in life.*

Pope Pius XI called it: "The greatest of all our privileges from the Mother of God, which extends even after death." And the great Marian Doctor of the Church, St. Alphonsus Ligouri, exclaimed: "If we do a little more than Our Lady asks, can we not hope that we will not go to Purgatory at all?"

It is Our Lady's promise, for fulfillment of just three conditions, to make us saints.

The Triumph

Thomas Fahy, who is one of the greatest experts (and one of the greatest apostles) of the "new and divine holiness," began with special devotion to Mary, living the Blue Army pledge. He is Vice Postulator in the United States for the cause of beatification of Luisa Picaretta through whom the message of the new and divine holiness was revealed.

Like Tom Fahy, many who pledge that "specific response" requested by Our Lady at Fatima might never imagine to what heights Our Lady would draw them through living that "magic formula" of holiness.

Consecration to the Immaculate Heart of Mary is the underlying Secret of that "magic formula" given to the world by Sister Lucia who was left in this world to reveal the fullness of Our Lady's message of devotion to Her Immaculate Heart.

This "magic formula," the Blue Army pledge, is a greater challenge to the new century than might first appear. It is a "specific response" not only to save mankind from self-destruction *but to lead mankind into the era of spiritual triumph.*

This Fatima pledge, this "magic formula," is *the door to the "new and divine holiness"* as we shall explain more at length. The *totus tuus* consecration is the "elevator" to this degree of holiness.

We step onto that elevator by responding "totally" to the conditions of this simple formula given to us at Fatima from Our Lady's Immaculate Heart.

Above is image of the "Sacred Heart" of Jesus and Mary designed by St. John Eudes, the apostle of the Sacred Hearts.

CHAPTER 7

What is Needed

The specific response.

We have been told that Our Lady has been able to hold back the chastisement because of the saintly few. Now *those few must increase in number* to bring about the "era of peace for mankind"—the era of the Two Hearts.

Dr. Tom Petrisko was right when he said that all the other messages from Heaven of this past century are like posters on the wall of Fatima saying, "Pay attention!" That wall stands before a sinning world with the words of The Mother: "Stop offending God Who is already too much offended!" We are, as Jean Guitton said, at the hinge of history!

She comes in the thunder of a great miracle, clothed in the sun. She comes "terrible as an army set in battle array."

For All Nations

The image, which "came alive" and spoke in the convent of the Handmaids of the Eucharist in Akita,

Japan, was a statue copied from the image of Our Lady of All Nations given in Amsterdam, Holland, some forty years before. It is an image of Our Lady standing before the Cross, Her hands extended downwards as on the Miraculous Medal.

She stands on the world pouring light of Mercy, peace, and justice on peoples of all nations.

This "Akita poster" on the wall crying: "Stop here!" has a new ring of urgency. At Fatima, Our Lady spoke of the annihilation of entire nations. At Akita, She speaks of a "chastisement worse than the Deluge" now at hand which will affect "a great part of humanity."

The statue of Our Lady of All Nations in the chapel of the Handmaids of the Eucharist in Akita, Japan. It was this statue which came alive and spoke. Later, it shed miraculous tears 101 times, in confirmation of the message.

The Lady of All Nations is not just repeating what She had said at Fatima. Now She is explicit. If the world does not heed these signs from God, *much of humanity will be destroyed by fire.* And She added the terrible words: "Those who survive will envy the dead."

The urgent need now is for daring and effective leadership in the Fatima Apostolate and a *united effort* to obtain from ALL Catholics the "specific response" to save mankind from self-destruction. This has been the driving motivation for the author's recent books *The Day I Didn't Die, God's Final Effort,* and *You, Too! Go Into My Vineyard!.*

The wall God put in our path at Fatima to save mankind from plunging forth to self-destruction is not only a wall that says: "Do not pass." *It is a wall on which are written, in bold letters, God's instructions for turning back.*

We feel that we cannot repeat too often the words of the Pope: *Fatima is one of the greatest signs of the times not because of the miracle but because it indicates the RESPONSE necessary for meeting the alternative now facing the world: "To save mankind from self destruction."*

Dwindled Pledges

Before the dissolution of the Soviet Union, twenty-five million Catholics had made that response in over a hundred countries. They were called "the Blue Army of Our Lady against the red armies of Satan."

During recent years, the "specific response," as the Holy Father named it, has declined from tens of thousands of pledges a year to only a few hundred.

We are speaking primarily of a movement that is entirely spiritual. It is not a "club" or special society. Bishop John Venancio,[36] second bishop of Fatima, emphasized the universality of this response to the call of Our Lady to ALL Her children throughout the world. He said:

> "The Blue Army asks nothing new in practice. The old devotional practices of the Church (Scapular, Rosary, Morning Offering) will suffice. It is for the Blue Army to make known to the whole world the message of Fatima, by all the means at its disposal, "so that all men of all nations will fulfill it in their personal lives."

But while it is a completely spiritual movement, which should be embraced by ALL Catholics, it has an organized part that promotes the message. This organized part was recently institutionalized into the Church with a new constitution through direct intervention of the Holy See. This organized part has an ever-increasing responsibility.

Is United Effort Possible?

After reading the above, Dr. Tom Petrisko commented: "I am not sure we understand the way things are going to be in the future. After I finished my book *The Last Crusade*, I realized that the last crusade transcended any one effort. This became especially obvious to me when I contemplated the millions of

---

[36] Bishop John Venancio, carefully chosen by the first bishop of Fatima as his successor, had been a professor of theology in Rome. The few words quoted here are from a pastoral letter of the Bishop which was published in the October, 1964 issue of the official publication of the diocese. The entire letter, several pages long, can be found in the book *Dear Bishop*, pg. 320-326.

conversions and the millions now praying the Rosary throughout the world today as a result of recent Divine interventions, in one of which Our Lady said She came 'to finish what I began at Fatima.'

"To me, all those who are responding are really Blue Army people whether officially or not. The Blue Army is a deeper reality now. The Blue Army's reality has exceeded its original concept."

Now Is the Time

After the "Great Event,"[37] when simultaneously all in the world will see themselves as God sees them, we may hope there will be many vocations to serve the Fatima Apostolate with *the sense of urgency* of making Our Lady's formula of holiness lived throughout the Church.

This formula of holiness is not for an esoteric few. To save mankind from self-destruction, it is a formula for all.

The Way Being Prepared

The threat of "fire from the sky" is not the only motive for universal response. Another is that *the great triumph is now almost within our grasp.*

Our Lady of All Nations, appearing in Amsterdam at the time Pope Pius XII first consecrated the world to the Immaculate Heart of Mary (1942), confirmed the promise of her triumph made at Fatima. She specifically promised the conversion of Japan.

The Apostolate in Japan, and the Korean Blue Army Sisters (already half a hundred strong and spiritually well-formed) may be a big force for imple-

---

[37] See the author's book *The Great Event*, published March 2000, concerning the expected worldwide illumination of conscience.

mentation of the Fatima message in Asia. The communities serving the Blue Army in the United States and in Italy are growing in numbers. The International Center of the Apostolate at Fatima may be used for inspirational seminars to train leaders for the Fatima Apostolate from all over the world.

Past efforts have already advanced us close to victory. The final victorious battle which finally, as Our Lord expressed it to St. Margaret Mary, will be to "wrest mankind from the dominion of Satan."

Vocations Needed

We stand in awe at the edge of these coming events. We wonder how all men of good will can be brought together like a united army, united in wielding the weapon of the "specific response." Although there is much promotion of the Rosary, *it is often without promotion of the important First Saturdays, without use of the Morning Offering for sanctification of daily duty*. And, although there is much said about the importance of consecration to the Immaculate Heart of Mary, there is little said (among other movements) of the use of the Brown Scapular, which Our Lady held out of the sky at the climax of the Miracle of the Sun. Sister Lucia included it, together with the Rosary and Morning Offering, as an integral and important part of the "specific response" with the statement: "As was said by Pope Pius XII, *it is our sign of consecration to Her Immaculate Heart*."

The laity must awaken to this responsibility. As the Pope said to the laity in *Christifideles Laici*: "You, too! have a responsibility in the Church."

How will the new century respond to the sad lament of Our Lady to Elizabeth Szanto: "I **performed a miracle at Fatima so that all might**

believe, and *how many have made the First Saturdays?"*

Awesome Responsibility

As I write this, to be read by most when I am no longer here, I tremble to think of the little I have done. I tremble even more to think of the failures. One consolation is that I never refused to go anywhere (even thousands of miles) to inaugurate First Friday/Saturday vigils. If I had my life to live over, the vigils would be a priority.

We must rejoice that the Alliance of the Two Hearts promotes them vigorously, especially in the Philippines. They are the best response to the message of Fatima and "God's Final Effort," as Jesus called it in those early apparitions to St. Margaret Mary. The world owes much to those who make the vigils and promote them in every diocese of the world.

Dear Mother, how will you judge us? Have too many of us, who know your message, been satisfied to fulfill it in a minimal manner, and without proclaiming your message to the world as you will have hoped of us? Since the Blue Army has been recognized by Rome as "The World Apostolate of Fatima," will the Eternal Judge hold us responsible for failing to fulfill this mission adequately?

Saint Faustina trembled when told that she would be responsible for many souls if she did not make known the message of Divine Mercy. How we must tremble for failure to fulfill and promote the message of which Our Lady said: "If people do as I tell you, many souls will be saved."

Oh, my dear Mother, you have warned us that God's Justice threatens to destroy a great part of humanity by fire. But is your triumph to be over a world of burned out corpses? May the message of *God's Final Effort* flood the earth![38] And may enough generous souls respond to bring about your triumph by Grace rather than by fire.

---

[38] *God's Final Effort* is a 1999 book based on these words spoken by Our Lord to St. Margaret Mary Alacoque. Published by the 101 Foundation.

CHAPTER 8

Our Lady Said: "Join The Blue Army"

Blue Army Pledge puts us on the ascent of Mount Carmel.

ONE OF THE GREATEST GIFTS from Our Lady to our age is the formula of Her "specific requests," which Sister Lucia coded into the Blue Army pledge. It is not only the way to avoid or mitigate the chastisement. It puts those who practice it on the ascent of Carmel. We find an example of this in *Don McBride's Journal*.

This *Journal*,[39] written over a period of two years, contains "conversations" of the writer with Our Lady, Our Lord, and saints such as St. Simon Stock[40] and St. Grignion de Montfort.

Most of the intimate conversations are with *Our Lady of Divine Love*, a title that was dear to Pope

---

[39] 106 typed pages, spiral bound, by Charles D. McBride, 335 Greene 443 Road, Marmaduke, AR 72443.

Pius XII and was especially popular in Rome during the Second World War. (There is a celebrated shrine in Her honor on the outskirts of Rome.) The devotion honors Our Lady as Spouse and Mediatrix of the Holy Spirit.

According to *The Journal*, Our Lady calls at this time for *prayer partners* to be keepers of the *Door of Love* (Her Immaculate Heart), the door between Our Lord and mankind. Through this "door" will come a New Pentecost.

In letters of introduction to *The Journal*, three priests who guided the author vouch for his holiness and credibility. His doctor (a non-Catholic) describes him as "sane and sincere." *The Journal* itself seems to confirm these judgments.

Began With Blue Army

Don, who was a convert from Protestantism, joined the Blue Army eight years after becoming a Catholic. He had lived his Blue Army pledge faithfully for 22 years, with ever-increasing awareness of his consecration to the Immaculate Heart, when the conversations began. Our Lady told him that it *was She who inspired him to join the Blue Army*. She loved him very much. *Now She wanted to get into "the very depths" of his heart.*[41] She wanted an act of total consecration.

---

[40] It was to St. Simon Stock that Our Lady gave the promise that whosoever dies wearing the Scapular will die in the state of Grace. Little is known of the life of the saint other than that he was, at the time of the apparition (July 16, 1251), the head of the Carmelite Order. The unusual devotion of the *Journal's* author to St. Simon seems to indicate special appreciation for the gift of the Scapular as a devotion of consecration to the Immaculate Heart.

Wearing the Scapular and saying five decades of the Rosary a day, he had, as already said, grown in awareness of his consecration to the Immaculate Heart. He had begun to pray frequently to St. Simon Stock, through whom Our Lady gave the Scapular as the intimate sign of belonging to Her.

Now suddenly, after these 22 years of devotion, he felt, within little more than two years, *Our Lady's Immaculate Heart become one with his,* lift him, in that short time, into the mystery of the Trinity and of Divine Love.

One With the Immaculate Heart

Our Lady said: "My love for you is true love. It comes from the very bottom of my Heart and it goes to your heart and entwines with your heart... Always remember to pray from the very bottom of your heart. Let all that true love flow out with your prayers. If you pray in this way, Our Lord will always answer your prayers."

Our Lady then asked for total consecration, introducing him to the method of St. Grignion de Montfort. To save souls, She needed prayer partners. She asked for daily Mass and Communion and monthly Confession[42] together with repeated acts of consecration to the Sacred Hearts.

He did as Our Lady asked and soon afterwards, She gave him *physical* evidence of the union of Her Immaculate Heart with his own heart. He writes:

---

[41] Pg. 57: "I was with you when you prepared to enter Our Lord's Church. I also directed you to join the Blue Army."

[42] For a time during the two years, Confession was made weekly, but the final request is monthly. One should follow counsel of one's Confessor.

"I could feel a strong movement around my heart, like a strong current in a river." He experienced a *physical warmth*, and felt that Our Lady was embracing him. Eventually this experience, frequently repeated, reached such a degree that on one occasion, he seemed not to be breathing of himself. Our Lady explained that Her Heart was so entwined with his that they were breathing together.

Union with the Sacred Heart

He speaks of the "entwining" of the Hearts of Jesus and Mary, and how hearts entwined with Hers entwine with the Heart of Jesus. This is perhaps the most precious message of *The Journal*. It is remarkably graphic.

From this time on, he seemed to leap forward in holiness and prayer life. Instead of five decades of the Rosary a day, he was now saying all fifteen, sometimes with even more Rosaries added.

"I could actually see Their open Hearts," he writes, "so beautiful! I could see flames going from one Heart to the other Heart." He felt his heart caught up in those flames of the Two Hearts.

Value of Prayer Group

"I want all My little children to join a prayer group," Our Lady said. "When you pray alone, you receive a certain amount of Graces. But when you pray, for example, with ten other people, your prayers will be ten times the amount you would gain praying alone."

St. Grignion, who was present with Our Lady, added: "Encourage them to pray together four to five hours a week. That is a small amount of time to give to our Mother who needs many Graces to accomplish the task Our Heavenly Father and Our Lord have given Her."

The saint added that, for these four to five hours, the Rosary was the best prayer. He suggested two complete (15 decade) rosaries, said with meditation *upon the mysteries as described in Scripture*, plus reading and discussion of Our Lady's messages, bible reading, and the fifteen prayers on the Wounds of Our Lord. He said the prayer group should not be "pushed" into such a full program. It should come little by little "because they *want to* do it."

Already thousands around the world follow this program, almost as St. Grignion describes it, *during the First Friday/First Saturday meetings and vigils* which have been promoted especially during the past half century by the Blue Army and which are a very important part of the Fatima Apostolate.

Other Means

Early in the 27 months covered by *The Journal*, Our Lady had asked that a room be set aside in the house as a prayer room. On a special table (altar), there was to be a bible, a rosary for each member of the family, pictures of the Sacred Hearts, a Crucifix, and holy water. On the wall, he felt inspired to place a picture of the last vision of Fatima.[43] (See picture next page.)

---

[43] This vision shows Our Lord on the Cross, surmounted by images of the Holy Spirit and the Father. Blood flows from the Head and Heart of Jesus to a Host suspended at His Side. From the Host, the Precious Blood drips into a Chalice. Our Lady, near the Host and Chalice, offers Her thorn-encircled Heart. Flowing "like water" down over the altar from the left Hand of Jesus are the words "Graces and Mercy." Pictures of the vision can be obtained from the Blue Army.

The final vision of Fatima in which the words, "Graces and Mercy" flowed like water down over the altar. It has been said that this picture represents the full message of Fatima, with its emphasis on the Trinity, the Sacred Hearts, and the Eucharist. For home shrines, a piece of the actual altar, over which the vision appeared, can be obtained free by sending a stamped and self-addressed envelope to LAF, PO Box 50, Asbury, NJ 08802.

This special room, or special place for prayer, was important. It was in this special room, after he had set it up as Our Lady asked, that he had the experience of seeming to be so *one* with the Immaculate Heart that He and Our Lady seemed to be breathing together.

Our Lord and Our Lady asked for acts of consecration to the Sacred Hearts, and that they be renewed often, by individuals and by families.

In addition to the Rosary, daily Mass, Communion, the First Saturdays (with monthly Confession), prayer groups, and becoming the prayer partners of Our Lady of Divine Love, Don was also asked to fast on Wednesdays and Fridays or to make some equivalent act of sacrifice and self-discipline. He voluntarily stopped smoking and reduced his use of alcohol. This was *without any forcing*. It came naturally with ever increasing love.

Padre Pio

The special patron and spiritual father of all Blue Army members is Saint Padre Pio.

In earlier years, Don had been on a pilgrimage to San Giovanni, where he attended the Mass of Saint Padre Pio who worked his spiritual "magic" on this simple Blue Army member.

Our Lady told him that *during the visit to Padre Pio, She had drawn close to him*. It was Padre Pio who had asked if one could do anything better than to make and keep the Blue Army pledge, and accepted all who kept it well as his spiritual children.

Also at the time *The Journal* began, when Our Lady was first manifesting Herself, Don was invited to go to Medjugorje. He hesitated until Our Lady told him that She wanted him to go, and that *he would find a confirmation there.*

One of the priests, most closely associated with the visionaries of Medjugorje, surprised him by suggesting *that he have a prayer room in his house with an altar bearing the very items Our Lady had told him to place upon it.*

Her Glorious Title

The two-year growth in holiness, which Our Lady asked to have recorded in this journal, is consistent with what is to be expected in this time of special

Saint Padre Pio at the offertory of the Mass. He accepted all who keep their Blue Army pledge as his spirtual chldren and prophesied the conversion of Russia "when there will be a Blue Army member for every Communist."

Grace and Mercy leading to the triumph. It is (as was said at the beginning) a confirmation of the message in the book *Her Glorious Title*.[44]

Already many souls in recent years, beyond our knowledge and counting, have been drawn up that mount of holiness, which we approach through the Blue Army pledge. Their number is known only to God.

It is certainly of them that Our Lady said at Akita that She has, because of them, so far been able to hold back Divine chastisement.

The Blue Army International Center at Fatima, showing top of major dome of Byzantine chapel, with "onion" dome and Russian-style cross atop it.

---

[43] *Her Glorious Title*, by John M. Haffert, is based on the last apparition in the Miracle of the Sun at Fatima—Our Lady of Mount Carmel holding forth the Scapular. It also explains the apparitions of Our Lady of Pellevoisin and the messages of Our Lady's *Flame of Love*. It is an urgent message for the hastening of the New Pentecost.

CHAPTER 9

Laity, Respond!

LAF: Holiness in the laity, our
hope for the future.

I N THE THIRD SECRET OF FATIMA, the Pope is
seen climbing the mountain through a half
destroyed city with "other bishops, priests,
men and women religious."

Conspicuously absent in the climb, up through
the ruins and over the many corpses, are the laity—until the Pope reaches the top. Only there *is
mention made of "various lay people of different ranks
and positions."*

And it is too late.

By the turn of the century, it had become overwhelmingly evident that progress to the triumph
depends much on spiritual formation of the laity,
especially of those apostolically involved in the life
of the Church.

For this reason, we inaugurated Blue Army seminars at Fatima and later launched the Lay Apostolate
Foundation. It was a response to the Pope's apostolic exhortation *Christifideles Laici* in which His

Holiness stressed today's urgent need for involvement of the laity in the life of the Church.

The vision of Our Lady preventing the Angel of Justice from setting fire to the earth shows that it is urgent. *There is a deadline.*

In his Angelus message of September 30, 2001, the Pope said:

"The terrible tragedy of last September 11 will be remembered as a dark day in the history of humanity... May God grant that *the faithful of the Church may be in the front line* in the search for justice, in rejection of violence, and in the commitment to be agents of peace.

"May the Blessed Virgin Mary, *Queen of Peace,* intercede for the whole world so that hatred and death may not have the last word!"

Immediately afterwards the Pope expressed his great joy that Luigi and Maria Quattrocchi would be beatified on October 21:

"Dear families, for the first time two spouses attain together, as a couple, the goal of beatification. For such a happy occasion I expect many to be present. This event is taking place twenty years after the publication of the Apostolic Exhortation *Familiaris Consortio,* which accented the role of the family, which in present-day society is especially downplayed."

Both quotations above are excerpts from the longer September 30 message in which the Pope dedicated *as many words to the beatification of two married lay persons as to the "terrible tragedy of last September 11" which "will be remembered as a dark day in the history of humanity."*

Pope John Paul II instructed the Congregation to concentrate on lay causes following the Council.

Most laypersons being forwarded for beatification were tertiaries of the various religious communities.

Models

Will the day come when we shall see images of laypersons in our churches? A model for doctors? (There is a saint.) A model for lay blacks? (There is a Blessed.) A model for single women? (There are at least two Blesseds.) A model for mothers? (Several are up for canonization.) A model for the various trades? (There are several!)

Indeed, models of heroic holiness are being raised up by the Church from almost every walk of life. But even though they are held before the laity of the world as their models, *they remain largely unknown.*

More will be said about this in the sequel to this present book, titled *To Shake the World.*

Today's Great Need

In his recent book, *The Dogma and the Triumph*, Dr. Mark Miravalle writes:

> "In an authentically Marian sense, we have reached the fullness of time. We have reached that which has been called the climax of the age of Mary, an apex, a summit, a high point which has been preceded by many holy events and great saints and teachers.
>
> "We who are consecrated as 'Totus Tuus' servants and slaves of our Mother Coredemptrix must now begin anew our prayer and labor for the Triumph of the Immaculate Heart of Mary! Even with the eventual definition of the last Marian Dogma, members of *Vox Populi* and all hearts consecrated to the Immaculate Heart of

Mary must continue to participate as a Marian family, a Marian remnant, in bringing forth all components of the great Triumph of our Mother, which lead to the Eucharistic Reign of the Most Sacred Heart of Jesus.

"We have a great responsibility, one which will not be easy to fulfill considering the state of the world and the many storms which rock the Church" (pg. 73).

Ultimately, the success of the lay apostolate will be the successful cooperation of involved laity "*in bringing forth all components* of the great Triumph of our Mother which leads to the Eucharistic Reign of the Most Sacred Heart of Jesus.*"*

Biggest Loose End

LAF (Lay Apostolate Foundation) was founded to be a catalyst for such cooperation. The officers who will determine its future will need many prayers. The book *You, Too!* will be a guide. We pray that the Blessed children of Fatima, Blessed Isidore, St. Benedict Joseph Labre, and all the growing host of lay saints, will inspire and assist those who will bring the lofty goals of LAF to fruition for the glory of God and the triumph of the Church.

In view of the release of the Third Secret, we should say a few words about LAF's principal goal: Lay vocations and holiness in the laity.

Marriage for Holiness

Although most laypersons are married, few seem to know that *the sacrament of marriage is a WAY of holiness*, and they lack some of the great aids to holiness (such as annual retreats) enjoyed in religious life unless they are acquainted with the Cursillo movement and other isolated examples.

Before the Second Vatican Council, which stressed holiness in the lay state, marriage did not seem to be perceived as a way of holiness in the same way as did entering a convent or a seminary.

In *You, Too!*, we find example after example of lay saints who, before becoming saints in the world, had first thought of entering a religious order or of becoming a priest.

This typical mindset motivated Grace McMahon, co-foundress of *Marriage for Holiness*, who had always wanted to be a nun. After the death of her husband, she began searching for the "right" community.

To her surprise, even though St. Paul advised widows and widowers not to remarry, after three years of preparation and search, her spiritual director told her:

"God wants you to remarry and help make known that *marriage is a way of holiness*."

Ten years into her second marriage, she said:

> "I am convinced that both the married state and the religious state have equal opportunities for holiness. *The opportunities are just different in each state. The married must be convinced of this or otherwise they will never aspire to the great sanctity to which God is calling them.*
>
> "The documents of Vatican II, *Lumen Gentium* and *Gaudium Et Spes*, make this point very clearly. We are all called to the same holiness. The only difference is the way we live it out. The mother making her life an oblation of sacrificial love, going to daily Mass and to adoration as her duties permit, is she not practicing heroic virtue?

"Vatican II opened wide the door to perceive the means for holiness in whatever the state of life to which we are called. What has been missing in the life of the laity is the special care given to religious formation and serious spiritual direction. Marriage must be seen as a *serious* means to perfection."[45]

While convent life offers special religious formation and spiritual direction, these can also be made available to the laity. There are also special advantages for holiness in the lay state in the "give and take" of marriage and family responsibilities. The fact that fifty percent of today's marriages end in divorce bears testimony to the opportunity for heroic virtue.

It will be remembered that when Our Lady asked St. Faustina to practice especially the three virtues dearest to Her, the most important was *humility*. The next two were *purity* and *love of God*.

One may even be proud of one's spiritual life. And marriage can be a MOST *valuable source of humility* for devout persons seeking perfection—perhaps *even more than in community life*, unless the latter is practiced with the childlike spirituality described by St. Therese of Lisieux, recent Doctor of the Church.

Recently, two married couples were comparing notes. Both were second marriages with children from the first marriages. This caused great stress, not just for a day but constantly for years. Almost every day brought repeated occasions for overcoming natural feelings of jealousy and even anger. There was constant need of seeking mutual understanding in the face of daily problems.

---

[45] Letter to the author, April 20, 2000.

By God's Grace

After years of dealing with these stresses, with faith and the strength of daily Communion, both couples said they were closer to God and had grown to love each other with a purer, disinterested love.

A wonderful example is found in the parents of Blessed Francisco and Jacinta, the visionaries of Fatima.

Olympia Marto, their mother, had two children by a previous husband before she married Tio Marto. Seven more children followed. Sanctifying their lives midst stress and responsibilities, Mr. and Mrs. Marto were worthy to become the parents of saints.

With frequent Communion and a sincere desire for holiness, the marriages described above—unlike so many which today end in failure—*fostered humility, purity, and love of God.*

I have personally experienced the great advantages for holiness in religious life: Ascetical training, holy companionship, blessed obedience, daily Communion and community prayer, days of recollection and annual retreats.

I also know from experience that marriage, when undertaken as a sacramental WAY of holiness, has advantages for holiness *proper only to the marriage state.*

Greater Difficulty

However, even though marriage is a particular way to holiness, and even though it is the sure way for those who are called to it, some special souls receive *a higher calling: To leave the world and to be consecrated entirely to God alone.*

Laypersons striving for holiness do not have a chapel and daily Mass in their own house. They do not have regular hours of prayer, which in some religious communities amount to several hours a day. They do not have regular ascetical training, frequent retreats, and a specific rule of spiritual life to which they bind themselves with a vow of obedience.

St. Therese of Lisieux, who was called to this higher vocation of total separation from the world in a cloistered community, understood that her vocation was to be *"the heart of the Church."* Once, St. Faustina exclaimed: "Oh, how sad it will be for the world when there is a lack of vocations to religious life!"

For this reason, while the Second Vatican Council insists on holiness in the laity, *it does not diminish the greater calling* of total dedication in religious life, so vital to holiness in the Church and to the salvation of souls.

The Challenge Now

Without diminishing the vital need for religious vocations, *the challenge flung to the new century by the Second Vatican Council* is holiness of the laity and *greater involvement of the laity in the life of the Church*. To extend some of the advantages of the religious vocation to the lay state, there is increasing availability of weekly prayer cells and vigils. Ascetical training is available in books and in annual retreats (such as those conducted by LAF).[46]

Holiness in Marriage

The married "rule of life," which has been canonized in saints like Blessed Anne Marie Taigi, was described by St. Paul: "Women obey your hus-

---

[46] These retreats are held for five days close to July 16. For information contact LAF, PO Box 50, Asbury, NJ 08802, www.layapostolate.com

bands—Husbands love your wives as Christ loves the Church."

It is a rule impossible to live to perfection without Divine help. But following that rule, *sacramented by Jesus as a WAY of holiness*, those who enter into marriage can become saints as great as any.

Blessed Anne Marie Taigi was told by God that she was chosen to give this very lesson to the world: the lesson of holiness in marriage. And not even St. Francis, St. Anthony, or many others of the greatest saints were more gifted than Blessed Anne Marie. She is the special patroness of LAF and the call to holiness in the married state.

Holiness in the laity and lay involvement in the life of the Church is the teaching of the Second Vatican Council. Its promotion is an important mission, largely unfulfilled.

The triumph requires that the mandate of the Second Vatican Council be fulfilled by active involvement of the laity in the life of the Church. *As Our Lady told us in Amsterdam: "The clergy are too few. Mobilize the laity!"*

Let us pray earnestly for those who will embrace this mission in the new millennium. The magisterium of the Church, in the Council and in *Christifideles Laici*, affirm it as the Will of God for the new times.

It is essential to the triumph.

The Blessed children of Fatima show the way.

Blessed Anne Marie Taigi, Patroness of young women and of marriage. She was accompanied by a light in which she saw current and future evnts. One of those future events was a worldwide "illumination of conscience" by which everyone on earth would see themselves as God sees them. She is the Patroness of the Lay Apostolate Foundation.

CHAPTER 10

Children Show the Way

Beatification of the children of Fatima throws new light on holiness of children. Their important role in "saving mankind from self-destruction."

NINETEEN YEARS TO THE DAY, before the day His Holiness beatified the children of Fatima, he was shot in St. Peter's Square. In his book *Crossing the Threshold of Hope*, the Pontiff wrote:

"**It seems as we approach the millennium, the words of Our Lady of Fatima are nearing their fulfillment.**"

These "words of Our Lady," nearing fulfillment at the millennium, were spoken to three little children. They are words which color the entire history of the world as it emerged from the bloodiest century in history into an era filled with hope by the promise: *"Finally My Immaculate Heart will triumph... An era of peace will be granted to mankind."*

Holiness of Children

Never before in history have any persons so young been raised to the altar. Children so young had never before been considered for sainthood because it was believed that they could not be old enough to have practiced heroic sanctity.

This glorification of two children is an historic milestone in the annals of the Church. It is another, and very important, effect of how Paul Claudel described Fatima: *"An explosion of the supernatural."*

After careful study of their lives, and the confirmation of miracles through their intercession, the Church decided that they DID practice heroic virtue. Not because Our Lady appeared to these very young people are they given the greatest of honors of the Church, but because the Church has come to the solemn decision that these two children are models of holiness.

This opens a whole new light on holiness in children and in the laity.

Two Children Very Different

These children now beatified, even though they are brother and sister who had a similar religious experience, are radically different.

Jacinta was preoccupied by the vision of Hell shown by Our Lady to the three children. She made heroic sacrifices "to save souls from going to Hell." She said she would spend her Heaven praying to save souls from Hell.

Francisco was preoccupied by the vision of the Eucharist in the light shining from Our Lady's Heart. Even though he received Communion only twice in his life (once from an Angel and once on his deathbed), he wanted always "to console the Hidden Jesus."

When he died, he said he would spend his Heaven consoling Our Dear Lord Who is so sad because He is so neglected in the tabernacles of the world.

Not all Catholics who lead lives of heroic holiness are beatified or canonized. Indeed there are very, very few. Usually it is because God confirms their lives with *miracles* because He Himself *wants to draw the attention of His Church to these special souls, the messages of whose lives are messages for each of us.*

When such "messengers" of God are raised to the altars, it is always to give models to the Church. It is always *to give a message of the ways to sainthood, the ways of holiness.*

The message given by the beatification of the children of Fatima is a message of holiness in youth, even of the very young. And it is a confirmation of *the message of Fatima itself as a way of holiness.*

It is the message *of hope for the world if we all respond with the heroism of these little children* who, when asked by Our Lady in Her very first appearance if they would be willing to accept whatever God chose to send them for the conversion of sinners, answered without hesitation: "Yes!"

The words of Our Lady of Fatima, the words of the promised triumph of Her Heart spoken to this heroic little boy and little girl, can come to fulfillment only if we, too, say "Yes" to what Our Lady of Fatima asks of us.

Special Grace

This is a special Grace for all of us in the world who are threatened by so much evil. It is a Grace, and an encouragement, for all those who strive to make known the message of Our Lady of

Fatima, to which these children dedicated their heroic lives.

"Oh how I love the Immaculate Heart of Mary!" Jacinta exclaimed. "How I wish all the world would love Her Immaculate Heart!" And little Francisco longed that all the world should be aware of the Sacred Heart of Jesus beating with so much love in every tabernacle.

The Church glorifies these children not so much because of what they saw and heard but because of what they did in response.

The beatification of the children of Fatima *confirms the message of Fatima as an authentic way of holiness for laypersons*. It confirms the message of Fatima as a way of holiness for persons in the world, even those as young as seven years old.

For the Apostolate

Obviously, this has tremendous implications for the Fatima Apostolate. Perhaps the Holy Father was aware of this when, despite very strong opposition from his advisors, he went to Fatima in person to beatify the children at the very place where Our Lady had given Her message of holiness to the world.[47]

In its March 2000 issue, *Inside the Vatican* featured the Pope's trip to Fatima with an opening question:

"Why is John Paul II traveling to Portugal on May 13 this year, five days before his 80th

---

[47] The only trip planned for the Holy Father in the Jubilee Year was to the holy places in Egypt and the Holy Land. The beatification of the Fatima children was scheduled for April in Rome. But the Pope, despite strong objections even from the Secretariate of State, insisted on beatifying the children in Fatima.

Blessed Francisco

birthday?... Why not celebrate this beatification in Rome? After all, it is the Holy Year when millions of pilgrims are visiting Rome..."

"John Paul is traveling to Fatima on May 13 because, as his pontificate nears its conclusion, he is seeking to say a number of important things to the world, to the Church, to Russia, to Europe, to Portugal, and to all men and women of good will.

"He is trying to make clear to the Church and the world that he thinks something very important happened in Fatima in 1917—something still very relevant today.

"He is trying to make clear that Fatima, like Mt. Sinai and the Holy Land (the only two other places to which the Pope traveled in the Holy Year) *is 'holy ground.'* (Emphasis added.)

We tend to focus on the extraordinary events of Fatima—the miracles, the prophecies. But the Holy Father said that what is most important is that Our Lady of Fatima has given us *the specific response needed to turn back the tide of evil in the world.*

What is most important about Fatima is contained in the Blue Army pledge, and in the First Saturday devotion and First Friday/Saturday vigils.

Now Our Models

In God's Providence, we have details of the lives of Francisco and Jacinta in the memoirs of Sister Lucia. Indeed, we owe the memoirs to them.

When the Bishop asked Lucia in 1941 to write about "what you remember about Jacinta," she began the memoir in which is revealed the first two

Sister Lucia before statues of Our Lady and her cousins shortly after the announcement of their beatification.

parts of the Fatima Secret. Indeed, so much was revealed in that memoir that she was asked to write about anything else she felt important to recall. This gave us the completion of the four memoirs, the "Fatima Bible," as we like to call that basic book on the Fatima events.

This now becomes an even more precious document because God has willed to hold up before us the example of the two children it describes, showing how they responded to what they saw and heard, showing how the simple message of Our Lady changed them in a matter of months into heroic souls willing even to face death in boiling oil rather than disobey Her.

"I Thought I Was About to Die"

Perhaps the most poignant moment in all the events of Fatima took place on the day the children were released from prison after having survived the ordeal of being told, one by one, that they were going to be plunged alive into a vat of boiling oil.

When I asked Sister Lucia how she felt after Francisco and Jacinta had been taken, ostensibly to be boiled in oil, she said: "I thought they were already dead...and that I, too, was about to die."[48]

Now, only a few hours after their release from the prison where they expected to die, Our Lady appeared to them.

Did She take little Jacinta in Her arms and say how proud She was of her? Did She put Her arms around little Francisco and thank him for being willing to die rather than deny Her?

---

[48] *Her Own Words to the Nuclear Age*, pg. 2. This book by John Haffert includes the full memoirs of Sister Lucia with commentary and additional facts. It is available from the 101 Foundation.

Instead, looking sad, Our Lady said: *"Continue to pray and make sacrifices. So many souls are lost because there is no one to pray and make sacrifices for them."*

"The world is on the edge of catastrophe," She said in Rwanda, where a million died a violent death when Her requests were ignored.

This is serious. Only She can save us from the catastrophe. *She asks our cooperation.* She chose little children to show us the way.

Oh, may those responsible for making Her message known realize, as did those little children, just how serious it is! May they realize how great is their responsibility!

May each of us, from the youngest to the eldest, say "Yes" to Her, as did Blessed Francisco and Jacinta.

CHAPTER 11

The New and Divine Holiness

Ascent of Mt. Carmel by *totus tuus* consecration. The era of triumph will be an era of saints.

S HORTLY BEFORE THIS present book about messages and events from the last century which challenge the new, we published a book about the illumination of conscience as experienced by St. Faustina and prophesied to be experienced throughout the world as a great moment of decision.

The book suggests that even before *The Great Event* (which is the title of the book), some who have responded to the message of Fatima *with total dedication are already living in the time of the triumph.* It says that the "new and divine holiness" can (and should!) begin in each of us NOW.

This new era of holiness began to show its light in the seventeenth century with the school of Cardinal de Berulle, Saint John Eudes, and the revelations of the Sacred Heart to St. Margaret Mary Alacoque, who called it: *"God's final appeal to wrest mankind from the reign of Satan."*[49]

The *totus tuus* message of St. Grignion de Montfort was given at the same time but did not begin to flower widely in the Church until this past century when it was held before the world by Pope John Paul II in his personal example, his papal motto, and in his encyclical *Redemptoris Mater.*

The flowering of the "new and divine holiness" has already been exemplified in recent saints like Saint Faustina and Blessed Dina Belanger.

Hugh Owen, in a recent book titled *The New and Divine Holiness*, predicts that it will become universal "in the near future." It is the climax of Fatima.

For those who have never heard of the new and divine holiness, it may seem like an impossible dream—like the lifting of the veil upon the already approaching glorious time when the prayer of two thousand years will be fulfilled: "Thy Will be done on earth as It is in Heaven."

Coming Soon

The way to experience this gift, as presented by the John Paul II Institute of Christian Spirituality, is fourfold:

1) *Total abandonment* to the Holy Spirit and to His spouse, the Blessed Virgin Mary;

2) An intimate *identification with the Hearts of Jesus and Mary*;

---

[49] See the author's book *God's Final Effort*, published by the 101 Foundation, January 2000.

3) An appreciation for the unique role of the Pope, and the clergy in union with him, in mediating the "new and divine" holiness to the Church and to the world;

4) *The full recognition of one's responsibility for participation in the imminent Triumph of the Immaculate Heart of Mary and the Reign of the Sacred Heart in the world.*

It is the triumph promised at Fatima, the triumph of God's Will fulfilled on earth as in Heaven. *And we can dare to believe that it can begin now, in each of us, if we believe enough to say "Yes" to the great gift God now offers to the world*, the gift of the "new and divine" holiness. It begins with a total consecration to the Immaculate Heart of Mary.

After Adam and Eve, She was the first to live in the Divine Will. Through Her, the original state of man living in the Divine Will, which ended with original sin, will be restored. It will be the time of *the fullness of the Redemption.*

Revealed to Saint Faustina

While the writings on this subject by Luisa Picaretta are still being evaluated, the wonder of the new and divine holiness is revealed in the life and experiences of Saint Faustina in the following excerpts from her diary:

> "Oh Jesus, pure Love! I do not need consolations. I adore You O Living Bread amidst the great drought in my soul. O Mighty One! Your Will is the goal of my existence. I am nourished by Your Will. (195)

> "Jesus Himself is my Master. He educates and instructs me. I feel that I am the object of His special action. For His inscrutable purposes and unfathomable decrees, He unites me to Him-

self in a special way and allows me to penetrate His incomprehensible mysteries. There is one mystery that united me with the Lord of which no one, not even angels, may know. And even if I wanted to tell of it, I would not know how to express it. I live by it and will live by it forever. This mystery distinguished me from every other soul here on earth.

"He looks with special love upon the soul who lives His Will. And Jesus told me that I was doing the will of God perfectly... He said: 'For this reason I am uniting Myself with you and communing with you in a special and intimate way' (603).

"Today I hear these words in my soul: 'Host pleasing to My Father, know, My daughter, that the entire Holy Trinity finds its special delight in you because you live exclusively by the Will of God. No sacrifice can compare with this (955).

"'You are the delight of My Heart. From today on every one of your acts, even the very smallest, will be delight to My Eyes, whatever you do'" (137).

Another Modern Example

Pope John Paul II raised another modern example of the new and divine holiness to the altars on March 20, 1993. Dina Belanger, after a brief career as a concert pianist and composer entered the convent where, after nine years in ever-growing holiness, she died at the age of 33. Her holiness began in childhood with simple devotions like the Rosary and the Brown Scapular. When she received the Scapular at the time of her first Confession, she said, "At once, I felt safe wearing the livery of my Heavenly Mother."[50]

---

[50] Autobiography, pg. 49.

When she was thirteen she chose as her motto "Death rather than defilement" and felt called to make the *totus tuus* consecration. We read in her autobiography:

> "I gave myself completely to the Blessed Virgin, through the practice of the perfect devotion called *The Secret of Mary* by Blessed Louis-Marie Grignion de Montfort. This complete abandonment of myself and all I possessed to the Queen of Heaven gave me much consolation."

However, it was not until years later, when she had entered into the "new and divine holiness," that she appreciated the power of that act of consecration. She wrote:

> "It is now that I understand just a little of how my good Mother has repaid me a hundredfold for this total offering. In Heaven, I will know what an advantage it has been to me to abandon myself completely to Her wise guidance. I wish I could consecrate all souls to Her, for it is She who leads us to Jesus; it is She that we must allow to live in us so that Christ can take the place of our nothingness; She is the safest, shortest, the most perfect way to lead us to the Infinite, to unite us with uncreated Love until we are lost in Him, immersed in the Source of eternal bliss."[51]

In those last words, Blessed Dina is describing the degree of holiness awaiting souls in the time of the triumph. It is truly, as Pope John Paul II said, a "new and divine holiness." On one occasion, Our Lord told Blessed Dina:

---

[51] Ibid., pg. 64.

"The Grace of My chalice is My Real Presence which I am giving you, as in the Sacred Host... You are constantly and really in possession of Me as during those few minutes following Sacramental Communion.

"My Power and My Goodness are infinite. It is as easy for Me to give Myself to you through an interior, intimate Grace that is apparent to no one as it is to conceal Myself in the consecrated Host... *Come into the essence of the Heart of God, into the very essence of the Divinity...* The greatest joy a soul can give me is to allow Me to raise Her up to My Divinity... I take immense pleasure in transforming a soul into Myself, in deifying it, in absorbing it wholly into the Divinity."[52]

The power of such a soul becomes "infinite."

Jesus said to Blessed Dina that the prayers and suffering she offered "*is of infinite value for souls.*"

Such an expression would have been considered "untheological" in the past as Hans Kung said to Sister Lucia concerning the words of the Angel: "By the infinite merits of...the Immaculate Heart of Mary."

We can understand them only when we understand what it means to "live in the Divine Will."

Indeed many have stumbled on those words wondering how the merits of the Immaculate Heart could be "infinite." But Sister Lucia answered with a simple question: "Perhaps the Angel did not know theology?"

We are nearing the end of the time of "God's final effort to wrest mankind from the reign of Satan" through the fullness of devotion of the Sacred Hearts. Jesus said to Blessed Dina:

---

[52] Ibid., pgs. 333-335.

"My Eucharistic Heart has two great desires whose ardor would cause It sudden death if It could still die: the desire to reign in souls through love, and the desire to communicate to souls the immensity of Its Graces.

"No invocation responds better to the immense desire of My Eucharistic Heart to reign in souls than: *Eucharistic Heart of Jesus, may Your Kingdom come through the Immaculate Heart of Mary.*"

Loose End

This brief chapter is to prepare and to alert the reader to this aspect of the triumph. I regret I will not live to see the fullness of its tide, but I rejoice that I have lived to see it begin.

I urge the reader to take in hand the book *Her Glorious Title* even though it seems proud for an author to recommend his own book. But I gain nothing in this world from it, and I am not proud for writing it. I am ashamed, having been inspired to write it, that I did not do better. I wish now I might have found a more compelling title for this wonderful message of Our Lady's Flame of Love, Which is Jesus.

As said above, this "new and divine holiness" will be the fulfillment of the Redemption when man will be substantially restored like Our Lady to the relationship with God that Adam and Eve enjoyed before the Fall. It will be a time of great and powerful holiness.

Will it flourish in a remnant, because the world will have failed to change despite the "great event?" Or will it dawn gradually, as already seems to be the case, becoming such a power of holiness that it will change the world by Grace? Many reading these words may soon know the answer.

Great spiritual power is already being unleashed in the world from the hearts of those who have embraced the new and divine holiness. At the threshold of the triumph of the Immaculate Heart, the Apostolate of Fatima bears a major responsibility in helping the world cross that threshold into this time of great spiritual power, this time of triumph of the mystery of redemption.

But we are only at the threshold.

The door is the Immaculate Heart. It is opened by the *totus tuus* consecration. When one is *truly* living in, by, and with Mary, one is already close to living in the Divine Will as She did.

Blue Army Pledge, the Threshold

St. Grignion De Montfort distinguished three phases of response:[53]

The first is that of ordinary practicing Catholics: "Fulfilling our Christian duties, avoiding mortal sin, acting more out of love than fear, praying to Our Lady now and then, honoring Her as Mother of God but without any special devotion to Her."

The second phase is the threshold to the door of Our Lady's Heart. St. Grignion de Montfort described it over three hundred years ago, and it is exactly the Fatima pledge.

The very words of the saint, written over three hundred years ago, distinguish this second phase with: *"The Rosary and the Scapular...honor Mary's images and altars, publish Her praises and enroll in Her Sodalities* (associations dedicated to Her, such as the Blue Army)."

---

[53] *True Devotion to the Blessed Virgin*, numbers 23-24.

The next phase, the door leading to the new and divine holiness, the saint describes as "known and practiced by very few persons. It consists in giving one's self entirely to Mary, and to Jesus through Mary, and after that *to do all that we do through Mary, with Mary, in Mary and for Mary.*"

It is so important a step in one's life that the saint suggests a thirty-three-day preparation for this act of total consecration, which may obtain for the soul the Grace of living in the Divine Will through Mary's life in the Divine Will. He says:

"This devotion is an easy, short, perfect and secure way of attaining union with Our Lord, in which union the perfection of a Christian consists. It is an easy way because it is the way which Jesus Himself trod in coming to us" (no. 152).

All our loose-ended concerns for the future of the Fatima Apostolate, and for the holiness of its religious communities and leaders, relate to our hopes for this new and glorious age of the fullness of Redemption.

The "specific response" given at Fatima is not only to save man from self-destruction, it is also to bring mankind into the era of spiritual triumph, the era of the new and divine holiness.

Msgr. Harold Colgan, in asking his parishioners in 1947 to make the pledge, asked that they wear an outward sign of blue, as a reminder to themselves and others, of their pledge. He thus challenged them to be *"The Blue Army of Our Lady,"* and that is how the Apostolate of Fatima received this name.

The Outward Sign

It is enough to wear a blue ribbon, but special pins are available. Those most commonly used bear the international symbol of the Blue Army: Doves in the form of praying hands holding the Rosary, and the words *Orbis Unus Orans* (One World in Prayer) in a circle between the strings of the Scapular.[54]

Some prefer the Blue Army ring because a ring on one's hand is a *constant reminder to the wearer* as well as to others, whereas the pin seems mostly a reminder to others. The ring bears the international symbol, described above, on its top. On each side, the Sacred Hearts are shown together on the globe of the world, surmounted by the Dove of the Holy Spirit, and bathed in His rays.

St. Grignion de Montfort recommended a chain bracelet as the outward sign of total consecration to Mary, of "holy slavery" to the Queen of the World. Today some might prefer the ring as equally meaningful and even more visible.[55]

Aids to Spiritual Awareness

The Scapular, the Rosary, the Morning Offering, the wearing of an outward reminder, are all *aids to awareness* that we are consecrated to the Immaculate Heart of Mary and seeking, *in union*

---

[54] This symbol was adopted in a meeting of international leaders of the Apostolate which took place in Germany in the middle of the last century (1951). It now appears on banners of the World Apostolate of Fatima all around the globe.

[55] It could be especially meaningful to begin wearing a sign like the chain bracelet or the ring at the end of the time of "total consecration." Husbands and wives might exchange bracelets or rings of mutual consecration to Mary as they once exchanged rings of consecration to each other. A priest or deacon, leading the ceremony, could be invited to place the bracelet or ring on those making the total consecration.

with Her Immaculate Heart, to hasten the triumph of the Sacred Hearts for ourselves and for the world.

Sooner or later, if we are *faithful* in living according to the "magic formula" as in the example of Don McBride, we shall be drawn to make the total consecration. The transformation will begin.

We can hasten it by increasing our personal sacrifices, such as periodical abstinence from things like sweets, alcohol, and tobacco.

Bud MacFarland Sr., a true expert on the message of Fatima and on "God's final effort to wrest mankind from the reign of Satan," particularly extols fasting. "Oh, what a blessing it is to have the Grace to fast (on bread and water) at least one or two days a week!" he exclaims.

At first, it seems difficult. We make excuses of age, or business, or concern about irregularity, or health, or whatever. But they are only excuses.

With that small leap of faith, we take a giant leap in the life of Grace. We will soon find ourselves saying with Mr. MacFarland, father of twelve and grandfather of some thirty and leading an intensely active life: "Oh, what a blessing it is to have the Grace to fast!" It helps us obtain the *great* Grace of "seeing through" the natural world into the three-dimensional world of God.

Now is the time of Mercy. It is not the time for excuses. Now is the time to "do what it takes" to open our hearts to what God wills for us in this third day of salvation history.

"On November 1, 2000 came astonishing news. Nikolai Sorokin of the Russia news agency Itar-Tass reported that the Icon of Our Lady of Kazan has not only been rediscovered, but that it is inside the Vatican—indeed in Pope John's private chapel—and that the Pope is seeking a way to return it to Russia.

"Because of all that the Icon of Our Lady of Kazan represents, the restitution of the Icon to the Russian people by the Pope would likely mark a dramatic step forward in the dialogue with the Russian Orthodox Church."

CHAPTER 12

The Icon of Kazan

Could this be a door to end the great
schism and to unite the Church?
Why did God entrust it to the Blue Army?

THIS BOOK ULTIMATELY PRESENTS, as the primary challenge to the new century, the need to respond to the Third Secret of Fatima with a new holiness to be achieved through total consecration to the Immaculate Heart of Mary. The power of this was witnessed in recent years in persons like Saint Faustina, who dared to ask that *"every single person who dies this day will be saved,"* and the *prayer was answered!* (See page 235.)

We are arriving at the triumph from a century of martyrs, a century of an "explosion of the supernatural," which has brought us this hope.

From seeds sown in the past, a harvest may now be gathered. From the seeds of national apostles scattered over the world can come a mightier army for the triumph of the Queen than the world has ever before seen.

126

One of the seeds of the past is the redemption of the miraculous Icon of Our Lady of Kazan to be one day returned to Russia, a nation deeply involved in the message of Fatima and in hope of the triumph.

Long before the Communist revolution, the Russians had a special liturgy for Our Lady of Kazan in which She was hailed as *"Thou who destroyest Atheism."*

For this reason the Communists *destroyed the Basilica of Our Lady of Kazan in Moscow* TO PROVE THERE IS NO GOD.

But the miraculous Icon itself, which had been carried at the head of the troops in all the major battles of the nation, had been smuggled out of Russia. It ended up in private hands. The Russian Orthodox Church in the United States raised money to purchase it in a nationwide campaign. When they had almost succeeded, the fund-raiser disappeared with the money. A second campaign was launched, and again the money was stolen.

Now the Orthodox[56] did not have the heart to campaign again to the same parishioners throughout the land. The Icon was about to be sold at auction when we learned of it (as described in Chapter 19 of the author's book *Dear Bishop*). We became convinced that it was God's Will that the Blue Army redeem the Icon so that it could be given back to Russia as a free gift in gratitude for the fulfillment of Our Lady's promise of the deliverance of Russia from an atheist rule.

[56] We refer to the Greek Orthodox Church which has valid sacraments but does not recognize the Pope as head of the Church. The Orthodox of Russia have great devotion to Our Lady and under Her title of Kazan, She is known as the "Liberatrix and Protectress" of Russia.

Basilica Rebuilt

After the dissolution of the Soviet Union, one of the first things the Orthodox did in Russia was to rebuild the Basilica of Our Lady of Kazan on Red Square. It was under construction when we went to Moscow in 1992 with a pilgrimage of almost a thousand, carrying the International Pilgrim Virgin, which left Fatima for Russia in 1947 and now finally arrived.[57]

The Icon was reserved in our beautiful Byzantine chapel at Fatima until shortly after the trip to Russia. At the request of the Holy See, it was suddenly transferred to Rome. It happened so quietly (perhaps for security) that even we who had been most instrumental in redeeming the Icon did not know about it.

We rejoiced to think that certainly this meant that the Holy Father would himself deliver it to Russia.

Shortly afterwards, when the President of the U.S. Blue Army, Bishop Sullivan, went to Rome for his *ad limina* visit, the Pope invited him to accompany His Holiness to Russia when he took the Icon back to the Russian nation. Perhaps the Holy Father intended that he would represent the whole

---

[57] There are two *original* International Pilgrim Virgin statues which left Fatima in 1947, one going towards Russia eastward and the other westward. The statue which finally arrived in Russia in October 1992, was the westward one which had been in the custody of the author from the very time it left Fatima in 1947. In the company of the Bishop of Fatima, it traveled around the world, to all continents of the world including a circle of the continent of Africa. It played a major role in freeing Poland from Communism. For full details, see the author's book *Finally Russia!* available from the 101 Foundation.

Blue Army and the sacrifices made by its members to redeem the Icon for this holy purpose.

God's Will

As told in our book *Dear Bishop*, after all the money gathered twice by the Russian Orthodox Church to redeem the Icon had been stolen, *we received an undeniable sign* that it was God's Will for the Fatima Apostolate (the Blue Army) to acquire it and return it (as a free gift) to the Russian nation.

It was valued at three and a half million dollars, which was a great sum at that time. But it was worth far more. The Russian Orthodox Archbishop of San Francisco, who had led the previous two campaigns to redeem the Icon, when asked its value said: *"It is priceless...priceless."*

We made the first payment from our personal life insurance policy. Afterwards, aided by Our Lady of Fatima and Her dear spouse St. Joseph (who had appeared with Her during the great miracle of Fatima), we did not miss a single payment.

Only at the turn of the millennium, shortly after the release of the Fatima Secret when the Pope asked all the Bishops of the world to join with him once again in a Collegial Consecration to the Immaculate Heart of Mary, did we begin to understand why God willed that the Fatima Apostolate should play such an important part in these events concerning Russia's most revered religious treasure.

Great Jubilee Event

On October 8, 2000, in the presence of some 1500 bishops, and *in union with all the bishops of the world,* before the statue of Our Lady flown from Fatima for this event, the Pope renewed the consecration of the world to the Immaculate Heart of Mary.

It was the first time so many bishops had been in Rome since the Council. (See picture on page 239.)

The Pope had previously made this consecration in union with all the bishops of the world on March 25th, 1984. It was soon followed by the end of the rule of militant atheism in Russia, as Our Lord had told Sister Lucia: "[The consecration] will end religious persecution in that country."

We could take this to mean the fulfillment of the promise of Our Lady of Fatima: *"Russia will be converted."*

The author, left, with the Most Rev. Tadeuz Kondrusiewicz, Archbishop of Moscow, on balcony of the author's apartment in Fatima, October 14, 1993. The previous day, anniversary of the Miracle of the Sun and of the sixth visit of Our Lady in the Cova (see Basilica in background), the Archbishop was the principal celebrant in the presence of more than 500,000. The ceremony was broadcast in Russia on the nation's major TV channel. It was later rebroadcast on the same day that the Soviets had usually held their annual mlitary parade and celebration in Red Square.

But is the end of the rule of militant atheism ALL that Our Lady was promising? Russia had millions of martyrs for the faith. It was the only nation outside of Portugal mentioned in the Fatima message. Were the liberated Russian people, with their great devotion and confidence in Our Lady of Kazan, to play a major role now in the coming triumph?

Our Lady had added directly *to the promise of the conversion of Russia* that there will be "an era of peace for mankind."

Did the Holy Father have this in mind when he renewed the consecration on October 8, 2000, in which the bishops of the Orthodox Church of Russia voluntarily participated?

Inside the Vatican, a magazine dedicated to Church events and papal messages, featured this consecration in its issue of November 2000.[58] (See picture on page 125.)

The opening lead of this issue, reporting the Jubilee Year collegial consecration to the Immaculate Heart of Mary, *was about the Icon of Kazan.* The following issue covered the history and significance of the Icon in depth. Following are some excerpts:

"Sometime nearly a century ago, the Russian people lost their holiest icon: the Icon of Our Lady of Kazan.

"Russia today is a country in waiting. Waiting to forget past cruelties. Waiting for a better future, which seems continually to be postponed.

"In 1918, the new Soviet government seized the Icon... *It vanished on the way* (between the time it was seized and its new destination).

---

[58] This excellent magazine is highly recommended. Address in the U.S.: New Hope, KY 40052.

"On November 1, 2000 came astonishing news. Nikolai Sorokin of the Russia news agency Itar-Tass reported that the Icon of Our Lady of Kazan has not only been rediscovered, but that *it is inside the Vatican*—indeed in Pope John Paul's private chapel—and that *the Pope is seeking a way to return it to Russia.*

"Because of all that the Icon of Our Lady of Kazan represents, the restitution of the Icon to the Russian people by the Pope would likely mark a dramatic step forward in the dialogue with the Russian Orthodox Church."

Inside the Vatican said that "on May 13, 1982, when the Holy Father came to Fatima for the first time after the assassination attempt to thank Our Lady for saving his life, he venerated the Icon of Kazan in the Byzantine chapel" (at the Blue Army International Center).

Perhaps the Holy Father has been thinking and praying about restoring the Icon to Russia ever since the Blue Army redeemed it with that intention.

Now Was the Time

But now was the time. *Inside the Vatican* said:

"He wants to do it himself, in person, before he dies. In May (2000), he turned eighty.... The situation is urgent. The clock is ticking.

"It is also ticking in Russia... The many injustices of the long and difficult transition from a totalitarian to an open society are leaving millions of Russians nostalgic for a past they have begun in some ways to idealize, exposing them to 'every kind of doctrine,' to charlatans and scoundrels of every type.

"In this sense, the Russians need the Icon of Our Lady of Kazan as urgently as Pope John Paul needs to give it to them.

The "Soul" of Russia

The full story in *Inside the Vatican* fills several pages explaining, as well as can be done, the extraordinary importance of this Icon in the history and devotion of the Russian people. It has been called "the soul of Russia." The article says "it is linked to the deepest sources of Russia's religious life...*it may be destined to play a pivotal role in the Christian history in the 21st century.*"

Author holding the Icon of Kazan in the Byzantine Chapel of the Blue Army International Center in Fatima. The Pope came here in 1982 to pay reverence to this image of the Patroness of Russia which he hopes personally to return to the Russian nation.

Following are some additional excerpts:

"Its return seems clearly connected with...consecration of the third millennium to Our Lady in front of the statue of Fatima on October 8 (2000) in St. Peter's Square in Rome.

"It is connected with the destiny of Russia as a nation.

"The theological meaning of the Icon is that Mary shows us the way towards The Way, Her Son Jesus... It *shows the way for the future of Russia.*"

Perhaps what is most amazing in the recent history of the Icon is that under Gorbachev, shortly before the change in Russia but while it was still supposed to have an atheist government, permission was given to build a chapel on Red Square in the place of the Basilica of Our Lady of Kazan which the Communists had destroyed eighty years before. *It was the first time permission was granted to rebuild a church under the Soviet regime.*

The implications of this are enormous. There must have been tremendous religious pressure building up within Russia ready to explode against the regime—and obviously centered on devotion to the Icon of Kazan.

Almost immediately after the dissolution of the Soviet Union, on November 6, 1990, the Metropolitan Alexei blessed the cornerstone for a new Basilica of Our Lady of Kazan to replace the chapel on Red Square.

On the eve of President Vladimir Putin's visit to the Holy Father in June (2000), in extraordinary circumstances time was given on Russia's national evening TV news (RIR) to explain what had happened to the Icon since 1904. The newscast reported

134

that the Icon was now in the possession of the Pope who would bring the Icon back to the Russian people. *Inside the Vatican* says:

> "There were reports of listeners being moved to tears to learn that the original had been found, and that the Pope wants to bring it back to Russia."

From July 2001 issue of *Inside the Vatican*: Archbishop Kondrusiewicz before the new Basilica of Our Lady of Kazan on Red Square, in its final stage of completion. It awaits the return of the Icon of Kazan, Patroness of Russia.

CHAPTER 13

"It Would Take a Miracle"

E VEN IN THE LIGHT of all that has been said, it would be difficult to grasp the depth of the devotion of the Russian people to Our Lady of Kazan. During all the days of the repressive Communist regime, it is said that there was hardly a home without the Icon, even if hidden.

When Pope Pius XII made the first consecration of the world to the Immaculate Heart of Mary on the 25th anniversary of the Fatima apparitions (1942), His Holiness mentioned *especially that nation where Our Lady's Icon lies hidden awaiting a better day.*

It is only now, after the end of the religious persecution in Russia, that we are coming to know the truth. The January 2000 issue of the *National Geographic Magazine* (pg. 14) published a picture of the image of Our Lady of Kazan *from the Russian space station Mir.* The Russian cosmonaut, Valery Ployakov, the man with the record for space flights, found support in having a copy of the miraculous Icon on his space flights. *National Geographic* reported: "The Icon is in his home, and *he carried a small reproduction of it with him on every space trip.*"

Following the collegial consecration of Russia to the Immaculate Heart of Mary, it would seem that the impossible has happened: *Russians and Americans work together on the new space station,* the successor to Mir.

Mir means peace.

"At the Center of the Struggle"

In his meeting with Pope John Paul II, Gorbachev, head of the Soviet Union, said: "Our biggest mistake was the repression of religion."

Many believe, as I did when I first held the original Icon in my hands with the intention of giving it back to Russia, that one of the great miracles of Our Lady of Kazan is that more than half a century after the Basilica in Moscow was destroyed by the atheists to prove there was no God and no Mother of God to protect Russia, the Icon had mysteriously disappeared from Russia and was now in the hands of the Fatima Apostolate—the apostolate in which millions in over a hundred nations had been praying for the "conversion" of Russia.

The lead article of *Inside the Vatican*, December 2000, reads:

> "As the year 2001 draws near, a spiritual contest of far-reaching proportions stretching from Rome to Moscow to Washington and touching many capitals in between, is being waged just out of sight of the world's press. It is a struggle with major implications for the history of the 21st century. *And at the center of the struggle is the little known Icon of Our Lady of Kazan.*" (Emphasis added).

An Aid to the Triumph

The article goes on to explain that a spiritual union of the East and West could halt the process of secularization, which has proceeded relentlessly during the past two centuries. It explains why the Holy Father wishes now to return the Icon to Russia:

"To lay down at least the initial bases for an eventual reunion between the Catholic and Orthodox Churches, separated since the 'Great

In March 2001, after 15 years in orbit, the worn out space station MIR plunged into the South Pacific. Recently, it became known that during the Cold War, a copy of the Icon of Kazan (Patroness of Russia, hailed as "Thou who destroyest Atheism") was carried on MIR by the Russian astronaut who spent the greatest amount of time in space. Now Russians and Americans serve together on the successor to MIR, which means "peace."

Schism' in 1054. The goal: To reunify the two largest branches of Christianity in order to face the challenges of the 21st century, and beyond, with renewed energy and faith. Indeed, John Paul seems persuaded that each branch needs the other: that the West needs the spiritual depth of the East, and the East needs the support and 'catholicity' that the West has to offer."

"It Would Take A Miracle"

We were given a clue as to the difficulty involved when the Holy Father went to Mount Sinai early in the Jubilee Year 2000 in the expectation of an ecumenical meeting with Orthodox and Muslims. His Holiness was longing for all to pray together, in the Jubilee Year, in basic solidarity of belief in the One True God. What happened shows that a great Grace is needed.

The Orthodox Archbishop refused to participate in the Mt. Sinai prayer. *The New York Times* reported (February 28, 2000):

> "Archbishop Damianos embraced the Pope as he arrived, but did not pray with him. '*It is impossible, it is against our canon law,*' the Archbishop explained later. He said that, for his faith, *unity between Roman Catholics and Orthodox was 'possible, but it would take a miracle.*'"

We can imagine the disappointment of the Pope who had made this ecumenical meeting high on the agenda of the Jubilee Year events. He had singled it out four years before in his encyclical *Tertio Millennio Adveniente*.

But in Moscow itself, due directly to the Icon of Kazan, a breakthrough had already been made.

The Orthodox Church Law, invoked to prevent common prayer with the Pope on Mount Sinai on February 28, 2000, *was waived in the Moscow Cathedral in 1992, before a copy of the Icon of Kazan, when the International Pilgrim image of Our Lady of Fatima arrived in Russia after 45 years "on the way"* from Fatima.

Our Lady of Victory

What happened in the Orthodox Cathedral in Moscow in 1992, before a miraculous copy of the Icon of Kazan, offers the hope that seemed dashed on Sinai.

As told in the book *Finally Russia!*, we began our trip from Fatima on the Catholic Feast of Our Lady of the Rosary (October 7), also known as the Feast of Our Lady of Victories. Ten days later, we arrived in Moscow with the Pilgrim Virgin on one of the major feast days of Our Lady for the Russian people, the *Feast of Our Lady's Intercession, also known as the Orthodox "Feast of Our Lady of Victories."*

The Orthodox Patriarch that same day met the leaders of the group and arranged for an historic meeting in the Moscow Cathedral on the following day with the Metropolitan Archbishop.

Praying Together in Moscow Cathedral

Before the crowd that packed the Cathedral, the Metropolitan said: **"We have known about the Blue Army. We thank all those who have prayed for Russia. During the dark years, the message of Fatima was our hope."** Then, he added:

"We know that the original image of Our Lady of Kazan is in Fatima and we look forward to its

Above, the Metropolitan Archbishop of Moscow addresses the crowded Moscow Cathedral (below). He said that all during the Communist years in Russia, through all the persecution, the message of Fatima had been their hope. He presented a framed image of the Icon to each of the leaders of the Blue Army pilgrimage and invited the chaplain, seen just to the right of the Archbishop, to pray with him before a copy of the Icon of Kazan. "We know the original Icon is in Fatima," the Archishop said. As he prayed together with the Blue Army group, it seemed that the thousand-year schism between the Orthdox Church and the Roman Catholic Church had been healed.

*return to Russia. We have a miraculous copy here
at which people have come to pray. Let us pray together before it."*

The Archbishop then invited the leaders of our
group up to the iconostasis (a screen separating the
sanctuary from the rest of the Cathedral) before the
miraculous image. *His Excellency presented to each
of us a small framed image of the Icon of Kazan.*
Then he said to our chaplain:

"Now I will say a prayer. If you agree, you will
say *Amen.* Then you will say a prayer, and if I agree,
I will say *Amen."*

Then followed a most fervent prayer from both,
followed by a resounding "AMEN."

*This may have been the first time in almost a
thousand years of schism of a solemn "praying together" of Catholics and Orthodox in the Moscow
Cathedral in a service arranged by the Patriarch.*

The Great Hope

What will happen when His Holiness carries back
to Her people the *original, miraculous* Icon of the
*"Patroness of Russia... Thou Who Destroyest Athe-
ism?"*

We in the West were privileged to redeem the
Icon. Now we are needed to embrace Russia with
our prayers as she receives back her beloved Patroness, her Lady of Victories as we consider the
following words from the *Inside the Vatican:*

"Secular observers in Washington, London
and elsewhere are wondering what cultural—
and thus political—influence Christianity will
have in the coming century. They both fear and
hope for a rapprochement between Rome and
Moscow. They fear it because they recognize that

a reunited Christianity could become the leading cultural force in the West and in the Third World, *halting the process of secularization, which has proceeded relentlessly during the past two centuries*, since the Enlightenment. And yet, they also hope for it, because the looming alternatives—a renascent China and a militant Islam—are both decidedly inimical to the 'Western project' carried forward by secular humanism."

Perhaps there has been no greater, single desire of the Pope in the Jubilee Year than ending the schism with the Orthodox Church. The Blue Army, which has placed the Icon of Kazan in his hands, has an added mission. Once again, its battle cry is for the "Conversion of Russia," but this time in a far deeper sense than just the end of militant atheism in Russia and the dissolution of the Soviet Union.

What Does It All Mean?

It is now our task to unite with the intentions of the Pope to fulfill what was started when the Blue Army and the Alliance of the Two Hearts took the Pilgrim Virgin to Moscow on the Feast of Our Lady of Victories only a few years ago. (To understand this better, please read the little book *Finally Russia!*.)

An archbishop and several other bishops of the Alliance of the Two Hearts also joined in that historic event in Moscow. We held an International Youth Congress in one of the newest and best auditoriums in the Russian capital which was joined by many, especially from various nations of Europe, who arrived in Moscow on their own.

This recalled that it was an International Youth Congress at Fatima in 1946, which set the Pilgrim

Virgin en route to Russia. *And when Our Lady's statue was crowned in Red Square, Our Lady was seen above the square, wearing a crown, with rays of light streaming down upon the square and then reflecting back up in all directions as though to illuminate the entire world.*

Of the thousand pilgrims who participated in this pilgrimage to Russia, almost all said they felt "called here by Our Lady." They prayed and fasted from Fatima to Moscow.

Through the Barriers!

Most were Blue Army members. Others were members and leaders of other apostolates, especially the Alliance of the Two Hearts. All were wearing blue jackets with the insignia of hands offering a heart to the Hearts of Jesus and Mary.

The main part of Red Square, in front of Lenin's tomb, was cordoned off and patrolled by soldiers.

To the amazement of the Russian guides, when our large group crowded against the barriers they gave way, and with tacit approval of the guards the thousand blue-jacketed children of Mary marched triumphantly over that pavement where for some 70 years atheist dictators had reviewed the might of the Red Army.

It was on the platform in the square, before Lenin's tomb, that they crowned the image of Our Lady of Fatima, who promised in 1917: "If my requests are heard, Russia will be converted and an era of peace will be granted to mankind."

Has the triumph begun?

Does it not seem that Our Lady is drawing all Her militant children together in this time of Mercy? More and more are joining the ranks. *More and more are making the total consecration.* Great spiritual power is beginning to be released on the earth, if not in great numbers at least in great holiness.

The Role of Russia

We know we experienced something extraordinary in Red Square on October 17, 1992.

The journey there with the International Pilgrim Virgin Statue had met great opposition, sometimes even by persons who should have been its greatest support. The struggle of spiritual warfare was never more evident. Yet, that journey of faith culminated before the miraculous copy of the image of Our Lady of Kazan in the Moscow Cathedral in an ecumenical service beyond our fondest hopes.

What does it augur for the future?

Russia was the only nation in the world, outside of Portugal, mentioned by Our Lady. She singled out this nation as a rod of chastisement for the world, and also a sign of Her victory: *"Finally My Immaculate Heart will triumph. Russia will be converted and an era of peace will be granted to mankind."*

At the beginning of the new millennium, it may seem as improbable that Russia could be an instrument of conversion in the world as it seemed improbable in 1917 that it could then have become an atheist threat to the world. But more than one believable voice is heard proclaiming that Russia will become a major force in Our Lady's triumph.

In any case, *Fatima and the Blue Army* (as the official Apostolate of Fatima) *are linked to Russia.* Those words spoken in Moscow by its Metropolitan Archbishop, as arranged by the Orthodox Patriarch, are springboard words of triumph.

He said that Russia had to acknowledge her sins, and during those dark years when millions died for the faith in a Russia ruled by atheists, *the message of Fatima sustained them in hope.* He thanked the Blue Army. He said they now longed for the day when the Icon of Kazan, the greatest of all symbols of Russian devotion to Our Lady, would come from Fatima back to the Cathedral, which they were already rebuilding, on Red Square.

What bearing does this have on the ultimate triumph promised at Fatima? What lessons is God teaching us from these events of the past century, the bloodiest century in the history of the world?

The grand finale of an already spectacular day (October 18, 1992), was the midnight crowning of the International Pilgrim Virgin Statue in Red Square by participants of the World Youth Congress.

CHAPTER 14

Turnaround

Holy Father Intervenes to Institutionalize the Blue Army into the Church.

RUSSIA'S "CONVERSION" was a principle motive for response to the message of Fatima during the many years that Russia's atomic arsenal posed a threat to the western world. The "cold war" constantly motivated us to fulfill the conditions for Our Lady's Promise: "Russia will be converted."

Now, with the dissolution of the Soviet Union, we seem no longer pressed by the threat of atomic devastation. We seem to be forgetting that the threat remains, and that the Fatima message bears Our Lady's promise not only of religious freedom in Russia but *also of the triumph of Her Immaculate Heart* with an "era of peace for mankind."

For whatever reason, in the last decade of the last century, interest in Fatima went into a major decline.

Why? One might ask how such an important message, bearing as it does the promise of the triumph of the Immaculate Heart, could cease motivating Catholics to respond. Pledges decreased from tens of thousands a year to almost none.

Similar reversals have occurred in other apostolates directly related to the triumph. Shortly after Saint Faustina received the Grace of the transfer of her own will for the Divine Will (374),[59] she had a prophetic vision that revealed:

> "There will come a time when this work, which God is demanding so very much, will be as though utterly undone. Then God will act with great power (action), which will give evidence of its authenticity. It will be a new splendor for the Church, although dormant in it from long ago.
>
> "God is infinitely merciful. He desires everyone to know this before He comes again as Judge. He wants souls to come to know Him first as King of Mercy. When this triumph comes, we (referring to herself and the priest assisting her) shall already have entered the new life in which there is no suffering.
>
> "But before this, your souls (including that of the priest assisting her) will be surfeited with bitterness at the sight of the destruction of your efforts. This will only appear to be so, because what God has once decided upon, He does not change. *But even though the destruction will be such only in outward appearance, the suffering will be real.*"

This prophecy was literally fulfilled twenty years after the death of the saint, despite the fact that

---

[59] Numbers in parenthesis after quotations relating to Saint Faustina throughout this present book refer to the paragraphs in *The Diary of the Servant of God*, Sister M. Faustina Kowalska, published by Marian Press, Stockbridge, MA 01263, edition of 1990.

Our Lord had told her that this message and devotion of Divine Mercy was necessary for the triumph. Jesus had told her:

> "You will prepare the world (with the message of Divine Mercy) for my final coming (429). For your sake, I will withhold the hand which punishes; for your sake, I bless the earth (431). Know that if you neglect the matter of the painting of the image and the whole work of Mercy, you will have to answer for a multitude of souls on the day of judgment" (154).

Yet after the "notification" by the Holy Office in 1958, the editor of her diary reports:

> "The images which had been hung in many churches were removed. Priests stopped preaching about the Divine Mercy. Father Sopocko himself (the priest who had assisted the saint) was severely admonished by the Holy See and suffered many other troubles in connection with the spreading of devotion to the Divine Mercy.
>
> "The Congregation of Our Lady of Mercy was also forbidden to spread the devotion. In consequence, the images, the chaplet, the novena, and all other things that might suggest that the devotion was being propagated, were withdrawn. *It appeared that the work of Mercy had been destroyed and would never rise again.*"

God permitted this to the very work He had said was a part of the key to the triumph of Grace in the world.

Perhaps one reason is that in the time of reversal, we evaluate our resources like an army in retreat, strengthening our resolve not to surrender and to do all that is necessary for victory. Perhaps another reason is to acknowledge that no work of

God depends on the instruments He chooses, but only on God Himself.

"Will Act with Great Power"

Saint Faustina said that when she was told by Our Lord that she would have to answer "for a multitude of souls on the day of judgment" if she neglected the picture and the work of proclaiming His Divine Mercy, "alarm took hold of me... So, I will not have to answer only for myself on the day of judgment but also for the souls of others! These words cut deep into my heart."

Our Lord consoled her by letting her know that after the apparent cessation of the work: "*God will act with great power, which will give evidence of its authenticity.*"

This happened when Pope John Paul II canonized the saint and on the same day (April 30, 2000) not only approved the work of Divine Mercy but fulfilled one of its principal conditions: The Feast of Divine Mercy.

New Hope

What happened to the apostolate of Divine Mercy also happened, to a large extent, to the Apostolate of Fatima. And again, it was the direct intervention of the Holy Father that saved it.

However, even after the papal intervention, which resulted in a new constitution institutionalizing the Blue Army into the Church, the rebirth was not immediate. But it was secure.

In 1999, I took it upon myself to write to the Blue Army leaders of some fifty dioceses:

"After the experience described in my book *The Day I Didn't Die*, I write in the hope of convincing you that the Apostolate must fo-

cus on the Blue Army pledge because it *is the
official response to the message of Our Lady of
Fatima, which the Pope has said was given by
God to meet the alternative now facing the world.*

"It is the MOST IMPORTANT APOSTOLATE
in the world, bearing as it does the promise of
the triumph of the Immaculate Heart of Mary.

"It deserves EVERY PAGE in its own, official magazine.[60] This is its only voice to those
hundreds of thousands out there who once
supported this Apostolate and have now fallen
away. It should be proclaiming to the world the
Pope's very recent message about the urgency
and importance of this 'specific response', which
is our vocation, and our responsibility, to
promote. And we now seem to be failing in this
responsibility.

"Where are we going to find persons with the
necessary charism—persons who see the importance of the Pope's Fatima letter concerning the
'specific response to save mankind from self-
destruction?' Who will we find who is alive to
this urgent message of our time upon which
depends war or peace, by Our Lady's own prophecies and promise?"

The membership responded. The leaders from
throughout the country, in a vibrant national meeting,
accepted the responsibility. They became involved
in the electoral process and passed several vital reso-
lutions.

---

[60] Reference is to *SOUL* magazine which was founded
to be the voice of the Blue Army but subsequently became
a "National Catholic Magazine" covering a wide variety
of subjects. As such, it was perhaps one of the best of all
the general Catholic magazines, but the Blue Army had
lost its "focused" voice.

It seemed that almost everyone knew action was needed. The spirit of that national meeting, at the dawn of the new millennium, seemed to come alive to the urgent need for the individual members to realize how much depends on each of them.

The new constitution which now governs the Blue Army, and which was given and approved by the Holy See through the instrumentality of Bishop Egan, now the Cardinal Archbishop of New York, places complete power in a few elected officers. The responsibility now lies on the individual members, down to the newest member of a parish cell to hold them accountable.

Turnaround

I sent an advance manuscript of this book, *Deadline*, to persons who could give advice for correction or improvement, including theologians and other qualified persons and experts in their particular fields.

A particularly capable leader of the Blue Army Apostolate, with over forty years of experience, suggested that one reason for the decline of the Apostolate in the United States was the spread of false rumors.

When I replied that, in view of the big turnaround in the 1999 elections, the rumors would dissipate in time, this experienced leader quietly insisted:

"Many will have taken years of silence about these rumors as confirmation. This has certainly contributed to loss of membership. You should not leave this world, as you seem to be doing in this book, without telling the whole truth."

The advice was well taken. At this same time, after a silence of two years, Father Roux, head of the Marian Movement of Priests in the United States,

Left, His Eminence, the Most Rev. Theodore McCarrick, Archbishop of Washington. Right: His Eminence, the Most Rev. Edward Michael Egan, Archbishop of New York. These two prelates were most instrumental in institutionalizing the Blue Army into the Church.

Archbishop Egan, while Bishop of Metuchen, communicated with all the Bishops of the U.S. and determined that over 50% had recognized the Blue Army in their dioceses. Authority of the Blue Army was then trasferred from the trustees of the Ave Maria Institute, Inc., to elected trustees of the Blue Army USA, Inc.

Archbishop Egan, on mandate directly from the Holy Father, made several trips to the US National Center in Washington, NJ and to the International Center in Fatima. Expert in Canon Law, he provided a new constitution to govern the apostolate nationally and internationally. He personally presided over the national meeting in which the constitution was adopted. Also present was the Most Rev. Constantine Luna, International President of the Blue Army recognized by the Holy See.

issued a bulletin to all the centers stating that there had been a major decline because of false rumors concerning Father Gobbi, the founder of their movement. The bulletin refuted the rumors in detail.

But concerning the Blue Army, another advisor (Dr. Tom Petrisko) wrote:

"I believe the past should be put to rest. I do not think the militant membership (of the Blue Army in the United States) went from 240,000 to 40,000 because of 'false rumors.' The drop is too great to be from organizational disputes."

Individual Responsibility

I decided to follow the latter's advice. The Blue Army has now been "institutionalized" in the Church. It has a new constitution put in place through the direct intervention of the Holy Father. The past is only important as a leaping off place.

But we must not forget that we are in a very real spiritual warfare. If we are not living Chapter 12 of the Apocalypse, as many believe, we are living an analogous time.

It is most urgent that the *individual members* of the Apostolate in each nation accept the *individual responsibility* this new constitution places on every militant Blue Army member throughout the world. Each one is responsible to elect holy and capable persons to direct the Apostolate in each diocese. Those officers, in turn, are responsible for the national and international Apostolate. And *every Catholic, in every state of life, has a moral obligation to respond to the message of Fatima, which the Holy Father says "compels the Church."*

Does not Our Lord say to *each of us*, as He did to Saint Faustina: If you neglect this responsibility, *"you will have to answer for a multitude of souls on the day of judgment?"*

Importance of Formation

As we said before, a major part of that responsibility is formation of lay leaders. Those who are elected to govern the Apostolate need to be informed and adequately motivated. As the Holy Father said in his apostolic exhortation to the laity, the principal mandate of the Second Vatican Council is for lay Catholics to be involved in the life of the Church, including evangelization. Our Lady of All Nations, the same "Lady" who came at Fatima and Akita, said: *"Mobilize the laity."*

Motivation for promoting the Fatima message abounds in books like *Dear Bishop, You, Too!*, *Her Glorious Title*, and *To Prevent This!*. It abounds in books like *The Last Crusade*. For mobilization, we have the "bible" of the Fatima apostolate: *Her Own Words to the Nuclear Age.*[61]

Although I am the author of most of those books, I do not hesitate to recommend them even if it seems self-serving. Most were written at the end of my life with no selfish motive. Even the publisher of the most recent books, Dr. Rosalie Turton, despite the fact that she committed tens of thousands of dollars to their publication, cares only for the message. Without hesitation, and without condition, she offered to have them put on a CD and on the Internet. When reminded of the great loss that would

---

[61] *Her Own Words to the Nuclear Age* is the title of the *Memoirs of Lucia* as edited by the author. This book also contains the notes of the official documentarian of Fatima, Rev. Joachim Alonso.

be incurred by her foundation if the thousands of books on hand were not sold, she said:

"All that is important is that the message be heard. God will look after all the rest."

We can take comfort in the comment of St. Alphonsus at the end of his life when he was nearly blind and one of his own books was being read to him. He interrupted the reading, forgetting that it was a book he had written, exclaiming that *he hoped everyone would read it*.

The Challenge

Some twenty-five million around the world made the Blue Army pledge and the Soviet Union dissolved without bloodshed. The challenge now is to build on the past to *achieve the triumph*.

The centers at Fatima and Pontevedra (frequently with empty rooms from November to May) are ideal centers for formation with the tools now available, which include videos and books in every major language. Each diocese can have its own formation program with exchange of books and videos at their monthly meetings. Good people will act if they are *informed* and motivated.

The following chapters offer reasons why all should feel, as does Pope John Paul II, that the message of Fatima "compels the Church." It is the message of the "specific response" needed for the triumph. It bears that great promise: "If My requests are heard... My Immaculate Heart will triumph and an era of peace will be granted to mankind."

CHAPTER 15

Tapestry of Victory

Russia, the Fatima Apostolate, and the Triumph. Bishop of Fatima, at the Dawn of the New Millennium, expresses Hope.

HE DEEDS OF OUR LIVES often look like knots and loose ends. When we get to Heaven, we will see that the knots and loose ends are the underside of a tapestry woven by God. When He shows us the *other side*, we will be amazed at the marvelous design He has wrought.

Can we look at knots and loose ends to guess the design of God's tapestry for the triumph of the Sacred Hearts?

We are keeping in mind that the triumph/prophecy of Fatima (the triumph of the Immaculate Heart of Mary) is a prophecy of the triumph of the Sacred Heart of Her Son. It means simply that *the triumph of His Heart* will be brought about in the manner He has ordained—*through devotion to Her Heart.*

Our Lady revealed to us that Divine desire: "God wishes to establish in the world devotion to My Immaculate Heart." God's desire *for this way to victory* must be our way.

Her Heart is the door to the Spirit Who became Her Spouse. It is the favored door to Her Son. She is Co-Redemptrix, Mediatrix, and Advocate.

Possible Role of Russia

As we said in Chapter Five, it seemed unlikely at the dawn of the new millennium that the Church might dogmatize Our Lady's role as Mediatrix, Co-Redemptrix, and Advocate, even though this is a condition of the triumph, perhaps even its final sign.

We have been given to believe that Russia (as explained previously in reference to the Icon of Kazan) will play a major role in this victory in the 21st century despite the chaos of Russia, following the dissolution of the Soviet Union.

Could Russia's solid devotion to the Theotokos (Mother of God) pave the way for acceptance of the role of Mary in God's plan of salvation by Protestants?

It seemed improbable in 1917, in the chaos of the Communist revolution, that this nation could "spread her errors *throughout the entire world*." It may seem even more improbable that she could spread *throughout the entire world* the devotion through which the victory will come.

But can we not see Russian Orthodoxy ending the East–West schism and playing a major role in uniting Christianity?

Two loose ends seem to hang close together: that of Russia's role and the words of Sister Lucia the day after the Pope made the first Collegial Consecration on May 13, 1982.

When asked if this meant that the threat of atomic war was over, Sister Lucia said: "The Blue Army will have much to do."

At first, one might have thought she meant that the 1982 consecration was incomplete because of Russia. But, after speaking with her, the Pope himself almost immediately perfected the consecration. He sent a second communication to *all the bishops of the world*, to whom he sent a copy of the entire consecration of Russia made in 1952 by Pius XII. He remade the consecration in union with all the bishops of the world on March 25, 1984.

It seems evident that Sister Lucia meant that *"the Blue Army will have much to do" AFTER the change that would now take place in Russia.*

Organized Effort

Apart from those almost spontaneous words of Sister Lucia, spoken at Fatima in the élan of the Pope's first major intervention, our common sense tells us that there must be some organized, concerted effort to bring about the triumph. And the only organized international effort recognized by the Bishops of Fatima and by the Vatican is the Blue Army.

On November 11, 1999, the Bishop of Fatima[62] said:

> "I hope that the good Christians who organize the Blue Army (World Apostolate of Fatima) on the national, international, or supranational level, are touching a cosmic dimension...at the

---

[62] Most Rev. Serafim de Sousa Ferreira e Silva.

national level with attention to small communities and to minorities."

"If this is done vigorously and effectively, I *am convinced* that all of the pastoral message of Fatima, all the organization of the message of Fatima, all that is mystical in the message of Fatima will be *at the service of man.*"

And this is the message to which God has attached the promise of the ultimate triumph: "an era of peace for mankind."

The bishop concluded:

"The Blue Army corresponds to a rich patrimony of ethical, dogmatic, humanistic, and religious values. We are speaking of a relationship of permanent *reconciliation of innocent peoples.*"[63]

To the change in Russia, and the loose end of Lucia's words that afterwards, "the Blue Army will have much to do," add *the loose end of the affirmation of the role of Mary*—a loose end dangling into the threat of division in the Roman Church after a century of militant atheism and post-Conciliar denigration of the role of Mary in Western Christianity.

---

[63] Emphasis added. The author would like to note that this strong and profound statement of Bishop Serafim was a surprise to the author. It followed upon a thirteen-year hiatus of support of the Blue Army in the Diocese of Leiria-Fatima after the death of the Most Rev. John Venancio. From that time (1987), there was no international president until, with the cooperation of Bishop Ferreira e Silva, a President was elected in November of 1999 in an international meeting at Fatima with direct intervention of the Vatican. It seemed almost a new beginning.

Only Through Mary

How will the chasm, which misunderstanding of Marian devotion creates between Catholics and Protestants, be crossed? It is a chasm that casts its shadow into the Church itself.

Devotion to the Immaculate Heart lends to devotion to the Eucharist. Light from Our Lady's Heart shone upon the children causing them to "feel lost in God." In that light they were acutely aware of the presence of God in the Blessed Sacrament and cried out: "O Most Holy Trinity, I adore Thee! My God, My God, I love Thee in the most Blessed Sacrament!"

Bishop Serafim (Bishop of Fatima) waving as Our Lady's statue is carried back to the Chapel of the Apparitions after the Pontifical Mass of May 13th in which the children were beatified and revelation of the Third Secret announced. The Pope is seen at the left. Shortly before, Bishop Serafim expressed the hope that the Blue Army would bring the message of Fatima to the entire world.

Devotion to the Immaculate Heart, through the Scapular and Rosary and the First Saturday Communions of Reparation, is the key to Her triumph. But the triumph will be Eucharistic. The triumph will be the reign of the Sacred Heart.

Ultimately, the Eucharist is the Sacrament of unity. *Our cooperation will enable the light from Our Lady's Heart to shine upon the world, blinding Satan and revealing the True Presence of Jesus in all the tabernacles of the world.*

Pope John Paul II said in his book *Crossing the Threshold of Hope* that he was convinced that the victory will come through Mary. This was confirmed at Fatima. It was confirmed in Amsterdam in the recently-approved title of Our Lady of All Nations.

On the eve of a First Saturday, Saint Faustina said:

> "I saw the Mother of God with Her breast pierced with a sword. She was shedding bitter tears and shielding us against God's terrible punishment. God wants to inflict terrible punishment on us, but He cannot because the Mother of God is shielding us. Horrible fear seized my soul."

Perhaps it is both God's Justice and Mercy that causes Him to "want" to inflict a chastisement upon the world. Our sins cry out for Justice, and the loss of souls caused by the tidal wave of evil in the world calls for its destruction out of Mercy for so many souls being lost.

But victory will come through Mary. That has been promised. It is certain.

What seems impossible to us is possible to God. He is weaving the tapestry of the promised victory. He knows the part Russia will play and the part each of us will play. He asks each of us to do the little, specific task He gives. He knows the service and value of every knot and loose end.

The words of Bishop Ferreira e Silva are practical as well as prophetic: "In each nation, the national Apostolate concentrates on the small communities and minorities. It builds up spiritual strength from person to person with the simple formula of holiness given to us by Our Lady of Fatima. It builds a Divine force, parish cell by parish cell, until what seemed impossible is reality."

In less than fifty years, twenty-five million made the Blue Army pledge before the collegial consecration of 1984, which resulted in the change in Russia. Imagine what can be done in the next ten years with new means of communication! (Because of its almost revolutionary importance, we will speak of this later.)

Springboard of United Effort

The above-quoted statement of the Bishop of Fatima, made less than two months before the new millennium, is in itself a springboard to the triumph. The bishop seems to be saying that past efforts of Satan to divide the Apostolate have been defeated. He is challenging his own nation of Portugal: "The World Apostolate of Fatima (the Blue Army) from a very small place in the west of Europe near the Atlantic, in a small country—the place of the apparitions, Cova da Iria, which means *kiss of peace*."

The Apostolate of Fatima has struggled against powers of darkness and human weakness for over half a century. Our own weakness and faults, as well as those of others, have hindered and even threatened its progress. May our faults of the past be lessons for the future! May accomplishments of the past be multiplied to hasten the promised triumph!

The change in Russia seemed impossible. The unity of all good Christians, in a concerted effort to bring about the triumph, may also seem impossible. But God has shown us the way in the thunder of a great miracle at Fatima, "so that all may believe."

The past can become a springboard to a united worldwide response to God's plan for the triumph. If we seize the moment, He will not fail to surprise us with His Merciful Love and Power.

Where we see loose ends and knots, He is weaving the tapestry of victory.

CHAPTER 16

New Battle Cries

The specific response! –Pope John Paul II
Could you do anything better? –Padre Pio
The triumph is ongoing! The Blue Army
will have much to do! –Sister Lucia

THE LEADERS AND WORKERS of the Apostolate today have immense advantages over those of the past century. In 1947, when the "march of pledges" was just beginning, the message of Fatima was virtually unknown outside of Portugal.

By the end of the century, millions around the world had made the pledge. The Pope himself was now the great advocate of the message. The two children of Fatima who had died not long after the apparitions were raised to the altars: *Blessed* Francisco and Jacinta. And the "spiritual father" of the Blue Army has also been raised to the altars: *Saint P*adre Pio.

New banners fly over Our Lady's spiritual Army. The first of those, based on the Third Secret revealing the Angel of Justice about to set fire to the earth, could be the words: **HELP PREVENT THE FIERY SWORD FROM STRIKING THE WORLD!**

Other banners can proclaim the recent words (1984-1997) of Sister Lucia: **FATIMA HAS JUST BEGUN! — WE ARE IN THE THIRD DAY! — THE TRIUMPH IS ONGOING! — THIS APOSTOLATE GIVES ME HOPE.**[64]

On another, beneath the image of Blessed Isidore: **THE SCAPULAR AND ROSARY MAKE SAINTS!** or the words of St. Dominic: **ONE DAY, BY THE ROSARY AND SCAPULAR, OUR LADY WILL SAVE THE WORLD.**

Another may proclaim the promise of Our Lady: **"AN ERA OF PEACE FOR MANKIND!"**

On another: **"THE SPECIFIC RESPONSE TO SAVE MANKIND FROM SELF-DESTRUCTION!"** –Pope John Paul II.

The words of Cardinal Tisserant: **"TO MAKE KNOWN, NOT ONLY TO CATHOLICS BUT TO THE WHOLE WORLD, THE MESSAGE OF FATIMA!"**

The words of Saint Padre Pio: **"COULD YOU DO ANYTHING BETTER?!"**

There could be *a host of banners* from all the words spoken by Bishop Venancio, the saintly successor to the first bishop of Fatima, such as: **"EVERYONE IS NEEDED IN HER BLUE ARMY!"**[65]

---

[64] The quotations have been slightly modified for brevity. The exact quotations will be found in Carlos Evaristo's book *Two Hours with Sister Lucia.*

166

Motivation

The importance of motivation cannot be over-emphasized. The battle cry of *Russia Will Be Converted* evoked greatest response when Communism, armed with atomic weapons, had engulfed a third of the world and seemed unstoppable.

In a recent book titled *Mary, My Mother and Queen,*[66] Kathryn Mary Williams writes that when she was a young mother of 28, with eight children under the age of 9, she attended a lecture on the spread of Communism. As the speaker put forth the facts and figures, she said:

> "The picture was too horrible to view. And we in the United States were sound asleep, not believing anything could ever change our beautiful and peaceful way of life.
>
> "I was visibly shaken. I was terrified by the thought that the future of my children could be menaced by these evil oppressors.
>
> "My first thought was, 'There must be something a mother can do to save her family.' And even though I was busy from morning until night, I thought: 'I've got to do something. But what?'"

Then she realized there was one thing she could do, even with eight little children. She could pray

---

[65] The lengthy message of Bishop Venancio to the Blue Army, issued in 1964, will be found in the book *Dear Bishop*, pgs. 320-326. This message of "Our Lady's Bishop" is too little known. It calls on ALL Catholics, in every walk of life, and ALL Catholic apostolates to realize that the Blue Army was raised up by Our Lady so that all apostles would have at their disposal its Church-approved local, national, and worldwide facilities to hasten the triumph.

[66] Published by *Queen of Peace Crusade*, 927 N. Silver Maple Lane, Peoria, IL 61604-4235.

the Rosary. She had said it for strength and help during pregnancies. "Now," she said, "it was for a totally different intention and purpose. I was praying the Rosary every day for peace." Only God could turn back the atheistic tide that was gradually bringing mankind to the point of self-destruction. She adds:

"Shortly after this, bits of information began coming my way—an article, a book, etc., and each with another clue to the mystery. I discovered that the Blessed Virgin Mary appeared to three little children in Fatima, Portugal in 1917 and told them to pray the Rosary to bring peace to the world... She foretold that Russia would be a threat to the world.

"I found the help I was looking for. The mystery was solved. I had found something that I could do to help bring peace to the world. I didn't know it then, but I had also found the Secret to peace for our own family."

Becomes Apostle

With the motivation of protecting the future of her children from the nuclear threat and the juggernaut of militant atheism, Kathryn Williams began to lecture in Church halls and schools.

As the years passed, her family grew at the rate of another child almost every year. Ultimately she had seventeen children! And her ardent apostolate seemed to increase in proportion to her family. At the end of her amazing book, she writes:

"I am encouraged by the prophecies of the great victory of Mary over Satan. I am motivated by my belief in the revelations given by God through Mary and Jesus.

"In 1966, Carl (her husband) was the construction superintendent on St. Joseph's Hospital in Bloomington, Illinois. It was time to dig the foundation. As I watched, standing on a hill of dirt, I marveled at the enthusiasm of Carl and those men. They were all so willing to do their jobs. They talked and planned and agreed on what to do. I said to myself:

"'Dear God, look at Carl and these men. They will work together to build this building. First the excavations, then the block layers, the iron-workers and carpenters, next the electricians, plumbers, and pipe fitters. Finally, all the other men who will complete this building. Carl has the blueprint and each of these craftsmen will come forward and willingly do their work. They will all cooperate and the result will be a beautiful new building.

"'And what about me? You, dear God, You are the Architect. I have read the blueprint. I understand it. It is the message Our Blessed Mother gave us a Fatima.

"'But how can I tell them. I need people to help me. I need workers who are excited about this blueprint who will work with me to make it known. I can't pay them, but dear Lord, You can! Won't you please help me?'"

A friend joined her and they launched a powerful local apostolate spreading the message, distributing hundreds of Rosaries and Scapulars, culminating in 1999 with the publication of her inspiring book.

Future Events

There are more and more apostles like Kathryn Mary Williams who often cry out in their hearts, "Who will help me?"

They can easily join or form diocesan divisions of the World Apostolate of Fatima. They can have a voice in the national council, reaching far beyond their local area. And a person like Kathryn could easily be elected to the national executive committee, actually commanding all the resources of the Apostolate throughout the nation. Even more, she could become a member of the international executive committee governing the Church-approved Fatima Apostolate in the entire world!

At the beginning of the new millennium, motivation of people to respond to the Fatima message remains hindered by widespread materialism. The vision of the Angel about to set fire to the earth seems remote. And if Our Lady has "so far" prevented the chastisement, why be concerned?

But, as we have mentioned elsewhere, there will be a sudden awakening when the very first terrorist use of an atomic weapon takes place, incinerating some part of the world as would have happened in New York with the bombing of the World Trade Center if the terrorists at that time had the "right" bomb.

"To Save Souls!"

At the moment, the major incentive is to save our children from the tidal wave of evil unleashed in the last century and devastating the new generation.

It was not primarily to save us from nuclear war that Our Lady gave us the "specific response" but to save souls. The key motivating words at the moment are, "So many souls are lost! *If people do as I tell you, many souls will be saved!*"

Unfortunately, people seem to fear loss of life and property more than loss of souls. That is why many think that at least limited chastisement, as in Bosnia and Rwanda, is in our future. That is why it is very important to look at those tragedies and then remember that ten years before they occurred, Our Lady warned that they would take place if Her message was ignored.

We recall again the words spoken to Our Lady by one of the visionaries in Rwanda: *"I know what makes you sad. It is because no one will listen to your requests until it is too late."*

Heroes to Lead the Way!

We cannot wait for further calamities to awaken the world to the reality and urgency of the Fatima message as it is proclaimed in the Vatican document on the Secret. We must act now with the new battle cries and with the glowing example of the children of Fatima.

Raised to the altars at the beginning of the millennium, they are in themselves heavenly banners calling us to fulfill Our Lady's requests.

We should read over and over *Her Own Words to the Nuclear Age*, the memoirs of Sister Lucia with all the notes of the official documentarian of Fatima and with special insights for the Apostolate. This is the true story of those heroic children. This is the basic book for formation of Blue Army leaders.

And the Church has recently raised up many other models of holiness in the world.

To do this subject justice, we would have to quote whole chapters from our book *You, Too! Go Into My Vineyard!*. But out of many examples, consider Blessed Isidore Bakanja.

Beatified shortly before the millennium, he was an ignorant convert from paganism—even more ignorant than the children of Fatima. He paid a great price for his conversion—separation from his family and his village. He paid a greater price for his apostleship—his life.

The Scapular he wore was for him truly Our Lady's own mantle, and it became a banner of apostleship. When asked what it was, he came aglow and told those working with him on the plantation about Our Lady, through whom the Savior came to the world, and that She had come from Heaven to take us under Her mantle that we might be saved. And he taught them the Rosary.

Blessed Isidore

This simple African *lived* the Blue Army pledge, and was its apostle. As we said above, the price he paid for his conversion was separation from his family, and virtual slave labor on a plantation. The price he paid for his apostleship was his life.

The atheist overseer said he was wasting the time of other workers and that he should take off the Scapular. When Isidore refused, the overseer tore it off, hit him with a whip, and told him not to wear it again.

Still smarting from the blows, after the overseer had left, Isidore picked up the Scapular and placed it again over his shoulders. The overseer then beat him so severely that, after suffering six months (during which he forgave the overseer and prayed for him), the young African boy died a beautiful death clothed in his Scapular, saying the Rosary. He was beatified in Rome in 1996.

New Love

I have accumulated some hundred relics but one, which I frequently use of late, is that of Blessed Isidore. Thanks to Blessed Isidore, I began to see Americans and Africans in a new light. I began to watch black evangelists on television with an open heart, and to marvel at the fervent devotion of their congregations. Such simplicity and faith!

How dear they must be to Our Lady whose favorite virtue is humility. And how sad that most blacks, at least in the United States, do not know Her. Like the children of Fatima, what power they would add in Our Lady's army to obtain the "era of peace for mankind!"

May Blessed Isidore inspire us, lead us, and intercede for us!

The Blessed Children

And what could be more humble than those children of Fatima who had not learned to read and write, one of whom (like St. Bernadette of Lourdes) had such difficulty learning Catechism that his first

Blessed Isidore

Communion from the hands of a priest was on his deathbed.

We tend to look down upon children as not as educated as we are. It is still difficult for us today to understand those words of Our Lord: "Unless you become like little children, you shall not enter the Kingdom of Heaven."

The Giant Who Frightened Lucia

The children of Fatima have a particular lesson to give us in holiness and humility. This was dramatically confirmed the day I asked a lawyer, who had been a leader of the brancardiers at Fatima for many years, what wonders he had witnessed at Fatima.

He was a giant of a man, seeming almost twice as tall as many Portuguese. He had first come to Fatima on an excursion from the nearby city of Torres Novas on September 8, 1917. Lucia tells us in her second memoir that she thought he was one of those persons with whom "grown-ups would try to frighten children." She writes:

"He was of such tall stature that I trembled with fear... I thought my last hour had come. My fright did not pass unnoticed by the young man who tried to calm me... He asked my mother to let me go and show him the site of the apparitions and to pray with him there.

"All along the way I trembled with fear... Then I began to feel tranquil again at the thought that if he killed me, I would go to see Our Lord and Our Lady...

"He accompanied me most of the way home and then he bade me a friendly farewell... I ran off helter skelter to my aunt's house, still afraid he might turn around and come back!

"What was my surprise then, on the 13th of October, when I suddenly found myself, after the apparitions, in the arms of this same person, sailing along over the heads of the people. It actually served to satisfy the curiosity of everyone who wanted to see me!"[67]

It served an even greater purpose.

There were tens of thousands of people there that day and they had just seen the Miracle of the Sun. Now "sailing" through the crowd on the shoulder of this gentle giant, as though high on a moving pulpit, Lucia cried out the words of which she said: "Of all the words spoken at this apparition, the ones most deeply engraved in my heart: *'Do not offend Our Lord God anymore for He is already so much offended!'*"

Lucia relates that later, "he appeared again... He came to thank the Blessed Virgin for the Grace received... This young man is today Dr. Carlos Mendes of Torres Novas."

What Impressed Him Most

As mentioned above, one day I met Dr. Mendes in the Cova and asked him to come over to the Blue Army house to speak to us about his experiences.

Being in charge of the stretcher-bearers, and having been in the Cova on the anniversaries of the six apparitions for more than twenty-five years, I knew he had seen many wonders. He was there on the occasion of two major miracles, which I myself had witnessed.

To my great surprise, he did not mention any miracles. He did not mention the visit of the Pope to Fatima. He did not mention the closing of the

---

[67] *Her Own Words to the Nuclear Age,* pg. 106.

Holy Year there or any other of the great and historic events he had witnessed. He spoke only of one event.

He said that when he first came to Fatima, he accompanied the children as they prayed the Rosary. Although in the years that followed, he had seen several major miracles, *nothing ever impressed him so much as the presence of Our Lady that he experienced while those children were praying the Rosary.*

They were *little* children. He was a *giant* in their eyes. They were illiterate shepherds of a lower strata of society. He was a lawyer of the upper class. But *in his entire life* nothing impressed him more than the way those children prayed the Rosary.

"A Child Shall Lead Them"

Can our sophisticated, highly educated generation pray to illiterate children for light and *guidance*, and imitate them? We know so much about geography, history, and science, but we have little of the humble faith which made those children saints.

As we have said before, they were not beatified because they saw the Blessed Virgin. They were beatified because *they did what She asked!* They were not raised to the altars alongside such doctors of the Church as St. Thomas Aquinas and St. Augustine because of what they had learned, but because of their *humility and holiness.*

Our Lady today would like us to fast on bread and water two days a week. Those children undertook total fasts while working in the hot sun, not because Our Lady asked them to do so but simply because She had told them: "So many souls are lost because there is NO ONE to pray and make sacrifice for them." The heroism of these *children* puts many of us to shame!

Oh, how we should hold up the banners of their example before our Blue Army members, and before the world! May God forgive us for the little we have done in this regard, and inspire those reading these words (especially those responsible!) with the firm resolve to do more.

Perhaps in addition to all the battle cries and slogans, there is an ultimate message which each of us should take personally to heart. It is the last exhortation of Blessed Jacinta to Lucia shortly before she died:

> "It will not be long now before I go to Heaven. You will remain here to make known that God wishes to establish in the world devotion to the Immaculate Heart of Mary. When you are to say this, don't go and hide.
>
> "Tell everybody that God grants us Graces through the Immaculate Heart of Mary...that people are to ask Her for them...and that the Heart of Jesus wants the Immaculate Heart of Mary to be venerated at His side. Also, tell them to pray to the Immaculate Heart of Mary for peace, since God has entrusted it to Her.
>
> "If only I could put into the heart of all the fire that is burning within my own heart that makes me love the Hearts of Jesus and Mary so very much!"[68]

---

[68] *Her Own Words to the Nuclear Age*, pg. 172, first published in 1993 by the 101 Foundation. It contains the entire memoirs of Sister Lucia interspersed with eight chapters of "comments" by John Haffert who considers this "the bible of Fatima." It speaks in detail of the lives of Blessed Francisco and Blessed Jacinta.

CHAPTER 17

Time of Mercy

As Our Lady holds back the fiery sword,
this present time is a time of Mercy.

W E CAN IMAGINE THE JOY Jesus experienced during His public life whenever He could be with His Mother. After walking the world with its sin and rejection, what joy and love when They met! What consolation Jesus experienced whenever He could return to the little house in Nazareth, *to the perfect love of His Mother.*

This is the consolation the *totus tuus* souls offer to Jesus at Communion, and with almost every act of the day.

The Angel instructed the children of Fatima:

"Pray! Pray much! *The Hearts of Jesus and Mary have designs of Mercy on you.* Offer prayers and sacrifices *constantly* to the Most High. Make *of everything you can* a sacrifice, and offer it to God as an act of reparation for the sins by which He is offended and in supplication for the conversion of sinners."

Our Lady came and *showed them how to do this by living in union with Her Immaculate Heart.* In hearts totally consecrated to Mary, the Sacred Heart finds the Heart of His Mother. When we make our hearts one with Hers, like St. John Eudes, we may hear Jesus express His Joy: "I have given you this admirable Heart of My dear Mother to be one with yours *that you might have a heart worthy of Mine.*"

Jesus told Saint Faustina that this is a special time of His Mercy. The spread of this *totus tuus* message is a special Grace of these times. There may be no single, more effective way to hasten the triumph than the *totus tuus* consecration.

From Bishop of Fatima

This time of Mercy is also a special time in which *Jesus reveals Himself as never before* in many personal revelations. The devotion of Divine Mercy, revealed in the diary of St. Faustina, is a most powerful new aid to holiness and to the triumph. Another is *The Poem of the Man-God* first published in the middle of the last century but just becoming known.

This book, to which we referred in Chapter 3, was recommended by a mutual friend[69] to the Most Rev. John Venancio, the Bishop of Fatima. I happened to be with the bishop in Rome when he purchased the ten volumes, then available only in Italian. It is one of the few books I know that has an *Imprimatur* by the Pope.[70]

---

[69] Rev. Andre Richard, D.D., author of many books, editor of the prestigious journal *L'Homme Nouveau,* and founder of the Blue Army in France.

[70] After reading it Pope Pius XII said: "Publish it as it is." The audience of the two priests who received this instruction from the Pope was published in *Osservatore Romano.*

Subsequently, when I met with the bishop, the conversation would frequently turn to the *Poem,* which the bishop was reading *every day.* He was an exceptionally well-educated spiritual man who had taught theology in Rome. He said that *appreciation of Jesus as the Man-God increased with every reading.*

Indeed Our Lord had said to Maria Valtorta:

"I was, I *am,* the Son of the Most High God. But I was also the Son of Man. I want this double nature of Mine, equally complete and perfect, to emanate very clearly from these pages... I am coming in this tragic hour (at the peak of World War II) *which are a forerunner of universal misfortunes,* to call back to your minds My double Figure of God and of Man, so that you may know It for what It is. Now you may recognize It after so much obscurantism with which you have concealed It from your spirits, and you may love It and go back to It and *save yourselves by means of It.* It is the Figure of your Savior. Whoever knows It and loves It, will be saved."[71]

At the same time, the book reveals Our Lady, in relation to Jesus, as a very real person. We come to *know* this Mother of our Savior as also our own personal Mother.

To describe how united His Heart was always united to the Heart of His Mother Jesus likened Their union to the "inextricable vines in an equatorial forest," which cannot be cut apart without cutting another—or "like the veins of a body, one alone of which cannot be deprived of blood because the same liquid fills them all." He likened His union

---

[71] Vol. 5, pg. 539.

with Mary to the union of a child in the womb to its mother, and said:

"She, oh! She, My pure Mother, bore Me not only for the nine months during which every woman bears the fruit of man, but for all of Her life. Our Hearts were united by spiritual fibers and they always beat together, and no motherly tear ever fell without leaving a trace of its salt on My Heart, and there has never been any internal moaning of Mine that did not resound in Her."

"That Wonderful Poem"

Although Italian was not one of my best languages, I bought the ten volumes and began to discover the wonder of this gift to our times. When the French edition came out, I had a fresh start. Finally, of course, we have it in English, and it is also available in other languages. I speak of it at some length here because I believe it is a very special blessing to the world in this "third day."

A few years ago as a Christmas present to the Holy Infant, I produced a booklet about the *Poem* as a gift to say, in some very small way: "Thank you, Jesus, for becoming *real to me as both Man and God* in these visions of Your Life."[72]

Father Roschini remarks that the *Poem* is new in that it sheds *new light on the old.* As a Mariologist, he noted: "besides restoring and completing the evangelical form of Christ, it also restores and completes Mary's." He added:

"Maria Valtorta not only makes the Blessed Virgin known to us, she also makes Her close to us. *She almost enables us to see Her as though we lived with*

---

[72] *That Wonderful Poem!* available from LAF or the 101 Foundation.

Her in gentlest intimacy. How I and other writers have described Her is like a *papier mâché* image compared to *the living person* revealed in the *Poem.*"[73]

Due, I am convinced, to Satan's effort, this very great gift to the new age remains still, to a large extent, undiscovered.[74] Indeed one marvels that so great a work could be so little known after Pope Pius XII said on February 26, 1948: "Let it be published as it is." The Pope was saying in effect: "It speaks for itself."

But we should not be surprised when we consider what happened to the work of St. Grignion de Montfort, buried for over a hundred years, and of St. Faustina whose works were "prohibited" by the Sacred Congregation in Rome in "notifications" of November 28, 1958, and March 6, 1959.

The Mercy Devotion virtually came to a halt. Only twenty years later, by the intervention of the new Cardinal of Cracow another notification, of June 30, 1978, declared the previous one "no longer binding." And still it was only after another twenty years, when that new Cardinal became Pope John Paul II and beatified Sister Faustina in 1998, that the devotion began once again to spread. But it still

---

[73] See introduction of the original Italian: *La Madonna negli scritti di Maria Valtorta,* published by Centro Editoriale Valtortiano SRL, Isola del Liri (RF), Italia.

[74] On January 6, 1960, a censure of the book appeared in *Osservatore Romano.* The officials who issued the censure were not aware of the declaration of Pope Pius XII on Febuary 26, 1948. Within weeks after this was called to their attention the censure was lifted *but still to this day that censure is quoted.* As Bishop Carinci, Secretary of the Congregation of Rites, put it: "The devil has too little in common with the Blessed Virgin." *Poema, IX, 219, note 69.*

remained virtually unknown in most of the world until April 30, 2000, when the Feast of Divine Mercy was instituted as Jesus had insisted as a condition for the triumph.

Much apostleship is required. We hope, from all we have said in the first few chapters, that this apostleship will be seen to be urgently needed.

So Few Know!

Three days before the canonization of St. Faustina and the institution of the new feast, this writer was on a transatlantic crossing by ship. He asked some twenty persons at daily Mass if they would like to share during the last three days, before the octave of Easter, in the Novena of Divine Mercy.

The passengers at that daily Mass were from all different parts of America. *Not one had even heard of the novena of Divine Mercy.* Even the chaplain, who was a truly good priest, did not know the name of Sister Faustina and did not know her canonization was scheduled three days later.

We who read books like this one presume that many others, like ourselves, know.

What a blessing it will be when the message of Mercy finally reaches those who don't know!

Perhaps that blessing will begin with the "great event." But it is the responsibility of each of us to open the way.

You Are There!

In the new time now coming, the *totus tuus* consecration will flourish, and writings like those of Luisa Picaretta and the *Poem* will be appreciated as a great blessing. Perhaps the latter will be especially valued by our separated brethren who so appreciate the Gospels.

What is so marvelous about these ten volumes written by the mystic, Maria Valtorta, is that she was "present" at the gospel events she describes. She makes the settings almost three dimensional, with colors and sounds and a variety of incidental details. We hear Jesus and the apostles *speaking*. We share in their intimate conversations. *We are there.*

Jim Tibbetts, of Two Hearts Productions, discussed with us the possibility of making *The Poem* into a motion picture. I pray that he will. Some day such a motion picture might become an even greater treasure than the book itself, making Jesus, together with His Mother, intimately known and loved by millions.[75]

What a time that will be, when the technology which has served the tidal wave of evil will be used to turn it back!

Recently a college in Texas produced a CD including "101 greatest Catholic authors." My book, *The World's Greatest Secret* happened to have been chosen as the 101st.[76]

How wonderful it would be if one of those comprehensive disks were available with great mystical and spiritual writings of our time, including the *Poem*, the ten volumes of which are costly and not readily available. Will such great treasures, such great spiritual gifts to our age, soon be available to all with the new technology?

---

[75] Jim Tibbetts, who has a master's degree in theology, is founder/director of *Two Hearts Productions*, 150 Holmes Rd., Scarborough, ME 04074.

[76] Our Lady of Corpus Christi College, Dr. David Marzak, Academic Dean, PO Box 9785, Corpus Christi, TX 78469. Email: Marzak@kolbefoundation.org.

One wonders, in this "third day," what marvels God still has in store for the world to enter the era of the new and divine holiness.

About the Chastisement

We read in *The Poem* the following words spoken by Jesus to His apostles:

> "You do not know the future. You consider great the sorrow now in the world. But He Who knows *sees horrors that would not be understood even if I explained them to you...* Never again will the Most High send universal calamities like the Deluge, but *men themselves will create scourges* that will be more and more dreadful, in comparison to which the Deluge, and the rain of fire which destroyed Sodom and Gomorrah, are merciful... Oh!..."

And Jesus made a gesture of anguished pity for that future time, which seems to be now.[77]

Immediately after Jesus said this, there follows a passage in *The Poem* which may help us to understand those mysterious words about Our Lady spoken at Fatima to our sinful atomic age: "Only She can save you."

---

[77] *Poem of the Man-God*, English edition of 1990, Vol. V, pg. 356.

CHAPTER 18

New Hope

The Great Event will be a moment of great Mercy. How could Our Lady's "specific response" prevent the chastisement?

A S WE SAID at the beginning, we have an obligation to remind all around us that chastisement will be inevitable before the triumph if men do not cease offending God or if we fail to make reparation.

We cannot insist too often on the terrible lesson of Rwanda. Our Lady foretold the terrible justice that would fall (river of blood, bodies without heads) if Her message was ignored. At the same time, She said: "I am concerned not only for Rwanda, or for the whole of Africa, but *for the whole world.*" And we recall again Her words:

"The world is on the edge of catastrophe."

We would wish all the world might know Her messages, as in the book *Too Late?,* which describes the apparitions of Our Lady in Rwanda and Bosnia.[78]

Her warning messages, given ten years before those countries were bathed in fratricidal blood, make us realize that the chastisement now threatening the world *has a time limit.* At the same time, they make us realize that God, in His Mercy, has sent Our Lady *"to prevent this."*

Indeed, "to prevent this" were Her very words, spoken at Fatima after the prophecy of annihilation of nations. The universal illumination of conscience will be a great sign of that Mercy which, if it evokes sufficient response, may prevent or at least mitigate the chastisement.[79]

Foretold for This Time

This great event, prophesied by Blessed Anne Marie Taigi, has in recent times been foretold as *imminent.*

Marie Julie Jahenny (born 1850) who was a stigmatist like Saint Padre Pio and *who foretold both world wars* long before they happened, said:

"If governments and political leaders continue to ignore and reject the sovereignty of God, there will be a severe chastisement which will change the face of the whole earth. Those few who survive will be charged with the responsibility to rebuild a world renewed in Christ.

"There will come a time and a *specific day close to the beginning of the 21st century when, by an Act of God, a grave and serious warning will come upon the whole world, an experience which every human being without exception will share simultaneously.*

---

[78] *Too Late?*, by John M. Haffert, available from the 101 Foundation.

[79] See book by same author *The Great Event*, published April, 2000, available from the 101 Foundation.

In the entire history of mankind there will never have been anything like it...totally without precedent."

This "great sign" and collateral miracles may be our last chance to avoid the chastisement.

God's Great Mercy

Some might think: "Well, let the chastisement come! It will clean out the world! What other way can we hope for the triumph of the Sacred Hearts?"

But Our Lady said this chastisement of fire from the sky will be *"worse than the Deluge"* because many souls will be lost.

She did not weep because of the chastisement itself. She said *She wept because "so many souls will be lost."*

We can presume, as we say elsewhere, that those who died in the Deluge had time to regret their sins. But the atomic weapons man has developed for his own self-destruction bring almost instant annihilation.

Why has Our Lady been permitted by God to come, as a loving Mother, "to prevent this?"

There is an episode in the *Poem* which throws light on this.[80] If not read as an authentic private revelation it is nevertheless a meaningful parable.

Divine Justice

Jesus is Mercy Incarnate. He forgave those who crucified Him. *He was always forgiving.* He was the *Savior.* In the more than 4,000 pages of the *Poem*, I can think of only twice when He acted as Judge.

---

[80] *Poem of the Man-God,* 1990 edition in English, Vol. 5, pg. 267. Available from the 101 Foundation.

One of those two times concerns a perverted, blaspheming, evil man who was feared by all his neighbors and who abused a little boy in his service.

A disciple of Jesus raised money to redeem the boy from the man's service. But the monster, whose name was Alexander, refused to release the boy after taking the money, denying that he had received it.

Three men in the village had witnessed the transaction, but they were afraid to testify. Jesus invited the elderly witnesses (one of whom was blind) to go with him to confront the villain. They apologized to Jesus that they had not testified before not only because they would have suffered retribution from the man, but he would have kept the boy anyway.

As Jesus and the three witnesses came near where the man was felling a tree, Jesus told the three, out of consideration for their fear, to stay out of sight. He called to the man who was wielding an ax: "Alexander!"

The Words of the *Poem*

"Who wants me? Who are you?"

"It is I, an Unknown Person Who knows you. I have come to take what is Mine."

"Yours? Hah! Hah! What is Yours in this wood of mine?"

"Nothing in the wood. In your house: Benjamin is mine."

"You are mad. Benjamin is my servant."

"One of my disciples gave you the money you asked to release the boy. You took the money and did not release him. My disciple, a peaceful man, did not react. But I have come in the name of Justice."

"Your disciple must have drunk the money. I did not get any. I am keeping Benjamin. I am fond of him."

"No. You hate him. You are fond of the money you do not pay him. Do not lie. God punishes liars."

"I did not receive any money. If you have spoken to Benjamin you had better know he is an astute liar. I will give him a good thrashing for slandering me. Good-bye!" and he turns his back on Jesus.

"Be careful, Alexander, because God is present. Do not defy His goodness."

"God! Hah! God to defend my interests? I only have to defend them and I do so."

"Mind you."

"But Who are You, You miserable Galilean? How dare You reproach me? I don't know You."

"You do know Me. I am the Rabbi of Galilee and..."

"Ah! Yes! And You think You can frighten me? I fear neither God nor Beelzebub. And You expected me to be afraid of You? Of a madman? Go! Away You go! Go I say. Don't look at me. Do You think that Your eyes can frighten me? What is it that You want to see?"

"Not your crimes, because I know them all. All of them. Also those that no one knows. But I want to see whether you do not even understand that this is *the last hour of Mercy* that God grants you to repent. I want to see whether remorse does not rise to split your stone heart, whether..."

The man hurls his ax at Jesus. The ax flies over His Head and strikes a young holm-oak that is cut clean and falls with a loud rustling noise of branches and whirl of frightened birds.

The three witnesses, hiding not far away, jump out shouting, fearing that Jesus might have been hit. The blind one cries: "Oh! to see! If I could only see whether He has been wounded! O Eternal God, my eyesight just for that!"

"I am all right, Father, touch me," says Jesus, reaching out to him and having Himself be touched.

Deprived of his ax, Alexander pulls out a knife and hurls himself at them to strike them, cursing God, scoffing at the blind man, raging like a wild beast.

But he staggers. He stops. He drops the knife. He rubs his eyes, closes them, opens them. Then he utters a frightful cry:

"I can't see any more! My eyes... Darkness... Who will save me?"

Strong Lessons

The above excerpt from the *Poem* teaches several lessons.

The witnesses, who were about to be attacked together with Jesus, laughed when Alexander was staggering about, blind. But Jesus at once said with His usual mildness: "Do not be like him. Do not hate." And He reached out and raised the head of the blind witness, the one who was so worried about Our Lord's safety. He spoke four words:

"Raise your head. Look!"

"I can see! My eyes! The light! May You be blessed!"

The old man stared at Jesus with his eyes bright with new life, then prostrated himself and kissed His Feet.

This was typical of Jesus Who was always merciful as He was as He warned Alexander: "I have come in the name of Justice... Be careful... God punishes... God is present... Do not defy His Goodness... this is the last hour of Mercy God grants you to repent..."

After the two words "last hour," *when Mercy was rejected,* the ax flew.

Most meaningful is what followed this incident when the holy women, who were accompanying Jesus at the time, were discussing it.

> Our Lady was silent, very sad.
>
> One of the women said to Her: "You would always forgive. You are so good. But justice also is necessary."
>
> "I would like nothing but forgiveness," Our Lady replied, "yes, only that. *To be bad must be a dreadful suffering by itself.*" And She sighed deeply.
>
> "Would you forgive everybody, really *everybody?*"
>
> "I would forgive. As far as I am concerned, I would forgive. *I see every soul as a more or less good baby*. A mother always forgives...even if she says, 'Justice exacts a just punishment'. Oh, if a mother could die to generate a new good heart for her wicked son, do you think she would not do that? But it is not possible. There are hearts that reject all help. And I think that pity has to forgive them as well. The burden on their hearts is already a very heavy one: the burden of their sins...and God's Justice.
>
> "Oh! Let us forgive guilty people! *May our absolute forgiveness be accepted to diminish their debt...*"

In the case of the wicked Alexander, Jesus left him in his blindness "that your soul may open to the Light." Even His Justice was Mercy.

But did those who died in the few minutes of the destruction of the World Trade Center in New

York, and in the Pentagon, have time to see the light?

Many must have saved their souls as they climbed higher and higher to escape the waters of the Great Flood, remembering the prophecies and warnings which had been given to them by God through His prophet Noah.

But the chastisement prophesied now will be "worse than the Deluge" because it may come at any time through weapons capable of wiping out entire cities in a single flash. The militants of Islam have some fifty atomic bombs in Pakistan. They have cells in sixty-four countries. We have already reached the deadline.

Even now, when mankind seems to reject the hour of Mercy as did Alexander, God sends The Mother to whom we were entrusted at the foot of the Cross. She comes with almost infinite pity offering the "specific response" (in the words of Pope John Paul II) "to save man from self-destruction."

This is the new hope.

193

CHAPTER 19

Adjusting to Change

Not all have adjusted well to the
changes in the Church. Eucharistic
challenge to the new century.

THE CHILDREN OF FATIMA were prepared for
the message of Fatima, with its terrible
prophecies and great promise, by the apparition of an Archangel bringing to them the
Eucharist. The Archangel prostrated before the
Blessed Sacrament, suspended in the air, and prayed:

> "Most Holy Trinity, Father, Son and Holy
> Spirit, I adore Thee profoundly. I offer Thee the
> most precious Body, Blood, Soul, and Divinity
> of Jesus Christ, present in all the tabernacles
> of the world, in reparation for the outrages,
> sacrileges, and indifference by which He is of-
> fended..."

In the past century, we quickly adjusted to the
replacement of horses with automobiles, paved roads,
skyscrapers, cinema, telephone, and radio. Then we
adjusted to television, computers, man traveling to

Space, and a host of other changes, which made this writer's century the era of greatest change in history.

But there were more serious changes in the area of faith and morals to which we have not adjusted so well. The most important of these are the changes in accessibility of Our Lord in the Blessed Sacrament.

Frequent Communion was just being introduced when the century began. My grandparents, who lived mostly in the previous century, could not accept that one could go to Communion even once without going to confession. Frequent Communion was only by permission of one's confessor. Children could not receive until they were "ready," and that meant sometimes even until the age of eleven or twelve. And we had to fast from midnight before receiving.

First Holy Communion was one of the best-prepared and most sacred experiences of our lives.

Oh, how we appreciated the True Presence of Our Lord in the Eucharist! How we trembled to think of receiving Him in a state of mortal sin! How much we appreciated this Sacrament of God's Love!

Only This Side of Heaven

St. Elizabeth Seton was consumed with a terrible thirst as she was dying. Water was offered to her after midnight. Because of the required fast she refused, gasping: "One more Communion, then Heaven!" *It was the Sacrament of Love, which could be received only on this earth.*

Many were deprived of Communion because of the fast. And children had to wait for years (and years to a child can seem interminable) to receive Jesus.

St. Therese, who reached the age of reason at three (from which time she said she never refused anything to God), had to wait until three times that age before she could receive Our Lord at all. St. Bernadette had not yet received her first Communion even when Our Lady appeared to her with a message for the entire world. Blessed Francisco of Fatima, although given Communion by an Angel, did not receive his First Holy Communion from a priest until on his deathbed when he was eleven years old. Yet the Blessed Sacrament was the central devotion in his life! (He said he would spend his Heaven consoling the "hidden Jesus" Who is so neglected in the tabernacles of the world.)

Blessed Changes!

Then the changes came. *Blessed changes!*

Children like St. Bernadette and Blessed Francisco and Jacinta could receive Holy Communion almost as soon as they reached the age of reason. The fast was reduced to one hour. DAILY Communion was not only permitted but encouraged!

Having lived all but fifteen years of the past century, and having been a daily Communicant from childhood, I can give personal testimony to the blessedness of these changes. Perhaps only those who lived through those changes, and who loved to receive Our Lord daily, can fully appreciate them.

Finally, towards the end of the century, when we attended a second Mass, we could receive Our Dear Lord a second time on the same day!

Time of Irreverence

While devout Communicants benefited by the changes, *some began to lose reverence for the Blessed Sacrament.*

Confession was less and less frequent. The less devout had already lost reverence when permission was given to receive Communion in the hand. And this seemed to add to the lack reverence.

The lack of reverence for the Eucharist is one of the most serious challenges now facing the Church. St. Thomas Aquinas says that the worst sins are those against the Eucharist because *they are sins against GOD in the very Sacrament of His Love.*

Our Lady said at Pellevoisin that what MOST offends Her Immaculate Heart are *careless Communions.*

We are rightly horrified by sins of abortion, all types of murder, torture of fellow human beings. But we seem to have lost our sense of horror for what most offends the Sacred Hearts: *careless Communions.*

So the Sacred Heart came, in what St. Margaret Mary called the final effort to save mankind, and asked for Communions of Reparation on the First Friday of nine consecutive months. Then His Mother, with Immaculate Heart pierced with thorns, came and asked for Communions of Reparation on five consecutive First Saturdays, and this time with mandatory CONFESSION, the Rosary, and meditation on the mysteries.

It was immediately after predicting the annihilation of entire nations if Her Fatima requests are not heard that Our Lady said: **"To prevent this,** I shall come to ask for...the First Saturday Communions of Reparation."

Sister Lucia says in her memoirs that Jacinta, unable to receive Communion because she was only seven years old, said: "From then on, whenever we spoke of this among ourselves, said: *'I am so grieved*

not to be able to receive Communion in repara-
tion for the sins committed against the Immaculate
Heart of Mary!'"

Heart of Fatima Message

Eucharistic reparation, including especially the
First Friday/Saturday devotions, has been a primary
subject in most of my books. I will not dwell further on it here. I presume that the average reader
of a book of this kind already knows that Eucharistic reparation is a primary need. Many are perhaps
already among the generous souls who make the
First Friday/Saturday vigils[81] and promote the First
Saturday devotion.

But it is important to address the very serious
problem of maladjustment to the changes in the
Church and the apparent increase in irreverence
towards the Blessed Sacrament.

Confusion

Although some of the liturgical changes are intended to facilitate frequent Communion and to foster
reverence for the Eucharist, Satan has used them
often to sow confusion and even irreverence. Certainly, this enemy of souls has sowed confusion over
the reception of Communion in the hand.

Recently a holy man, a daily Communicant for
many years, told me:

"When I understood that the hand was as sacred as the tongue I began receiving in the hand
as the pastor requested. Afterwards I would kiss
the spot two or three times out of reverence for where
Our Lord had rested the moment before Commun-

---

[81] See the author's book *Night of Love*, available from
the 101 Foundation.

ing with me. But then I heard that it was wrong to receive in the hand. I don't know what to do."

An old priest told me: "Oh, I am so glad for the change! My eyesight is failing and I used to worry in giving Communion, but now it so much more secure to place It in the recipient's hand!"

Some time later, I read in the diary of St. Faustina that one day the Host fell, as she was about to receive, but It landed in her hand. This was, of course, before the Church permitted Communion in the hand and the saint waited until the priest (who had continued down the rail distributing Communion to others) to return. She had not dared pick up the Host with her other hand. The priest did so and gave It to her.

Afterwards, Our Lord told her: *"I delighted to rest in your hand."*

Why? He delighted to rest in her hand because She adored Him there. She thanked Him for those precious extra moments of intimacy.

It is not that Communion in the hand *in itself* is wrong. But *careless* reception of the Eucharist in the hand, *ignoring the norms* for this *option*, is wrong. It is very wrong.

Mother Teresa of Calcutta once exclaimed that one of the things which most saddened her was the way Communion was received in the hand. It would seem that suddenly an almost indifferent carelessness, with which Our Lord is often received, was suddenly made apparent.

Church Does Not Mislead Us

The Instruction Concerning Worship of the Eucharistic Mystery, *Inaestimabile Donum*, prepared by the Sacred Congregation for the Sacraments and

Divine Worship and approved by Pope John Paul II on April 17, 1980, says:

> With regard to the manner of going to Communion, the faithful can receive it either kneeling or standing, in accordance with the norms laid down by the Episcopal conference: "When the faithful communicate kneeling, no other sign of reverence towards the Blessed Sacrament is required, since *kneeling is itself a sign of adoration.* When they receive Communion standing, it is strongly recommended that, coming up in procession, they should make a sign of reverence before receiving the Sacrament. This should be done at the right time and place, so that the order of people going to and from Communion is not disrupted (136).

The *Ceremonies of the Modern Roman Rite*, concerning the Eucharist and the Liturgy of the Hours states in Paragraph 336, after quoting the above norm of the Congregation:

> In our Rite, a "sign of reverence" to the Eucharist would be a genuflection or a bow (for one who cannot genuflect). This act of reverence before receiving Communion standing is easily planned and does not delay the reception of Communion. The person immediately behind the one receiving the Eucharist makes the reverence while he or she is receiving the Lord.

Inaestimabile Donum says this act of reverence is *"strongly recommended."* Fr. Vermeerch, S.J., a member of the Congregation, said this means we are to comply *unless there is a very good reason* for not doing so. When permission for the Scapular medal was granted, the decree strongly recommended that the cloth Scapular continued to be used. This meant there should be a *serious reason* for the substitution.

The Church did not COMMAND that we must bow or kneel before standing to receive Communion because there might be reasons why it might not be possible or convenient. But a good Catholic would certainly obey the *spirit* of the norm and make such an act of reverence before receiving Holy Communion other than on one's knees.

If one uses the option of receiving in the hand, even *added* signs of reverence are needed.

In addition to a genuflection (or bow), one is to receive on the left hand, placed over the right. Then one must step to the side, face the altar, look at Our Lord in one's left hand as one then places the Sacred Host in one's mouth with the right hand, looking at the same time to be sure there are no Particles remaining on the left hand. And then one returns to the pew to continue thanksgiving.

Receiving in this manner the communicant obviously adds additional acts of reverence.

But still it is obvious that the greatest reverence is given when we kneel to receive, and there is less danger of lost Particles if one receives on the tongue.

Proper Use of the Option

New norms have been issued by the Church as this book was being written. They deal with the abuse of the tabernacle being out of sight, of the failure to use a paten in the distribution of Communion. The priest is no longer to leave the sanctuary for the sign of peace. The new norms reaffirm the great reverence to be shown to the Blessed Sacrament.

God is with His Church. With time, due reverence for the Blessed Sacrament will be restored.

Meanwhile we must charitably point out that some options have been presented as "preferred" when they are not. They are simply "options."

We might suggest the example seen at the Blue Army Shrine in Washington, NJ.

At the weekday Masses, kneelers are provided for those who would like to kneel to receive. Communion is not refused to those who prefer to stand or who prefer to receive in the hand. But *it is made convenient to kneel and to receive on the tongue.*

Pilgrims coming from near and far almost invariably prefer to kneel.

But on Sundays and big Feasts, when there are crowds at the Shrine, Communion has to be given in various parts of the Shrine and the kneelers are not practical. This offers the advantage of the option to receive standing, remembering of course that *the liturgical norm requires that we show reverence by genuflection or a bow* before receiving.

The great success of Satan has been the confusion he has been sowing in the Church, often over questions which are not essential but which touch the very heart of our faith: the True Presence of Our Lord in the Blessed Sacrament.

When the modern liturgy suggested special chapels for the Blessed Sacrament, to the amazement and confusion of many of the faithful, the tabernacle was removed to a side altar in small churches where such a chapel was not practical.

Little by little, good sense seems to be returning. In the 1999 Conference of American Bishops, the majority of Bishops were overwhelmingly in favor of a prominent position for the tabernacle. As we said above, new norms from Rome are requiring this.

Some churches are even restoring use of the Communion rail.

The Essential

What is essential is awareness of the True Presence of Our Lord in the Eucharist with consequent reverence as shown by the Angel at Fatima.

Liturgical changes intended to facilitate reception of the Eucharist *must be adequately explained.* When they are optional, the choice of the communicant must be reverently accepted *and facilitated.* And this defense of reverence for the Eucharist is part of the mission of the World Apostolate of Fatima because reverence for the Eucharist is an essential part of the Fatima message.

This is evident not only from the apparition of the Angel with the Blessed Sacrament *occurring before* the apparitions of Our Lady, but also, during the apparitions of Our Lady, light shone from the Immaculate Heart upon the children, making them acutely aware of the True Presence, causing all three to cry out simultaneously:

"O Most Holy Trinity, I adore Thee! My God, My God, I love Thee in the Most Blessed Sacrament!"

Encyclicals

Are we being distracted from the urgent call of the Sacred Hearts for Communions of Reparation on First Fridays and First Saturdays? Are we being distracted by nonessential matters from what is essential to end the tidal wave of evil engulfing our children and calling upon the world Divine Justice?

When we see the entire congregation receiving Communion while only a few go to Confession regularly, are we moved to make Communions of Reparation? When we see Communion received with irreverence or indifference, are we moved to make

First Friday/Saturday vigils with Communions of Reparation to the Hearts of Jesus and Mary?

Are we being distracted (adding to our distraction with gossipy complaints) to the extent that we may not be seeing the great need of following the wishes of the Sacred Hearts? Are we even distracted by nonessentials to the extent of not reading and following the teaching of the Church updated to our times by the papal encyclicals?

So far, we have been speaking only of the need of restoring reverence for the Blessed Sacrament as a great need in the new century, but to some extent connected with this is the need to restore both *reverence and obedience to the voice of the Vicar of Christ* which is the *Voice of Jesus* to the Church in our times.

Jesus Speaking to the Church NOW!

While we pay much attention to liturgical changes, how much attention do we give, for example, *to sins against the Spirit, "for which there is no forgiveness?"*

Those sins are exposed in the encyclical of John Paul II on the Holy Spirit. They are the sins of those who parade the streets claiming the RIGHT to commit sin.

Encyclicals and Apostolic Exhortations are the Voice of Jesus to today's Church. **They are the voice of the Vicar of Christ speaking with authority.**

How clear they are! How forceful! Even though they are sometimes slow in coming (as in the case of *Humane Vitae*), the guidance is sure and true. And we can be sure that Voice will clarify the questions on the Eucharist, always asserting the Dogma of Transubstantiation. Meanwhile, just the encyclicals of the past century offer all the clarity and guidance needed to defeat Satan and to bring about the triumph.

If the Church had obeyed the encyclicals of Leo XIII on the Rosary and the Sacred Heart, the intervention of Fatima would not have been necessary. It was because the Church was not listening to the Vicar of Christ that His Mother came to perform a miracle "so that all may believe."

If the encyclicals of Pius XI and Pius XII on the Sacred Heart and on the Queenship of Mary had been followed, *we would already have the triumph.*

Today it seems almost as though the Vicar of Christ speaks in vain. Criticism of his voice is heard. The actual encyclicals are virtually *unknown.*

Inaccessible?

Early in the new millennium (March 2000), a client entered the largest Catholic store in a major metropolitan area and asked for recent encyclicals. The lady at the desk did not know what an encyclical was. She suggested that the priest on duty in the liturgical section (where they sold vestments, liturgical books, etc.) would know. So the client went there to ask.

Sorry, this largest Catholic store *serving an area of millions of Catholics did not carry ANY encyclicals.* When the client asked where they might be obtained, the priest said he would find out if the client came back in a few days.[82]

Is it any wonder Our Lady comes now as the Lady of All Nations, the Queen of the World, the

---

[82] Encyclicals can now be found in their entirety on several websites online including www.vatican.va and www.etwn.com, among others.

Mother of the Church, virtually shouting the word: *Encyclicals! Encyclicals!?*

In the apparitions in Amsterdam, the word ENCYCLICALS appeared in great capital letters as Our Lady stressed their urgency and importance. She also said: "The clergy are too few. Mobilize the laity!"

The world would not need apparitions, confirmed by miracles to make us believe, if the encyclicals were studied and obeyed. And one could say the same of liturgical norms, with options taken as *options*.

Let us not fall into Satan's snares of confusion. We honor and obey our priests and bishops with peace of heart, but in every circumstance with greatest reverence for the precious Sacrament of God's Love.

Eucharistic reverence is at the very heart of the coming triumph.

CHAPTER 20

WE WILL LONG FOR HER IMMACULATE HEART

"I have given you this admirable Heart of
My dear Mother so that you might have
a heart worthy of Me."
— Words of Our Lord to St. John Eudes

I N THE VATICAN DOCUMENT on the Secret,
we find the following statement in the theological commentary by Cardinal Ratzinger (Prefect
of the Congregation for the Doctrine of the Faith):

"There is a link between the charism of prophecy and the category of the "signs of the times,"
which Vatican II brought to light anew: "You
know how to interpret the appearance of earth
and sky; why then do you not know how to interpret the present time?" (Lk 12:56).

"In the private revelations approved by the
Church—and therefore also in Fatima—this is

the point: *They help us to understand the signs of the times and to respond to them in faith.*"

It may be some time before the Church in general is aware of the importance of these signs of the times, and especially of the enormous emphasis on the Eucharist given in the approved apparitions of Akita and Fatima, both of which are linked to the Angel with fiery sword.

At Akita, light shone from the tabernacle, causing the visionary to prostrate herself, in deep awareness of the True Presence. Her miraculous cure of total deafness, the final and great sign for the Bishop of Akita of the authenticity of the apparitions, took place at the moment of Benediction of the Blessed Sacrament. Praying with Sr. Agnes, Our Lady stressed the word TRULY in the special prayer of the community which Our Lady prayed with her. "Before *'present* in the Blessed Sacrament'," Our Lady said, "say *'TRULY'*."

At Fatima and Akita

At Fatima, God sent an Angel with the Blessed Sacrament. He taught them to pray: "I believe, I adore, I trust and I love You!" and: "O Most Holy Trinity, I adore You profoundly, I offer You the most precious Body, Blood, Soul and Divinity of Our Lord Jesus Christ, present in all the tabernacles of the world, in reparation for the outrages, sacrileges, and indifference by which He is offended..."

Afterwards, in light from Our Lady's Heart, the children were lost in God. In that light, aware of the True Presence, they were inspired to pray together: "O Most Holy Trinity, I adore You! My God, My God, I love You in the Blessed Sacrament!"

The last vision of Fatima, depicted in the picture on page 90, seems to summarize the entire message: the identification of the Mass and of the Eucharist with Calvary, the participation of the Godhead, the role of the Sorrowful and Immaculate Heart of Mary, and the flood of Mercy and Grace we can expect when we enter into this great mystery with faith.

Even though ultimately it is a gift from God, to obtain that faith requires effort on our part. We must ponder the words of Jesus, "This is My Body." We must use our hearts as well as our minds to embrace this seemingly impossible miracle.

Two Helpful Examples

In the book, *The World's Greatest Secret*, it is suggested that other miracles may help us, at least in a vague way, to understand this greatest of miracles, the Eucharist.

To test St. Bernadette, during one of the apparitions at Lourdes, a lighted candle was placed under her folded hands to see if she might react. She did not react to the flame. The candle was there long enough to burn her, but she was not burned. When the ecstasy was over, there was no mark on her hand.

Did her hand cease to be subject to the effect of fire? Did the flame of the candle cease to be a real flame?

What happened, quite simply, is that the EFFECT of the flame was SUSPENDED in relation to the saint's hand.

As explained in *The World's Greatest Secret*, it could be that in the Eucharist, the effect of the counter points of force in the Body of Jesus are suspended, making it possible for His entire Body to be present in the smallest particle.

A quite different example is found in another miracle that also took place at Lourdes. Like the suspension of the effect of fire on the hand of St. Bernadette, it was witnessed by many.

Dry Rain?

The custodian of the medical center at Lourdes, who remained to serve at the Sanctuary after being cured of lung tumors, sometimes experienced walking in the rain at Lourdes without getting wet. She didn't talk about it to many because it was so unusual. She called it "walking between the raindrops."

On a cold day in early November, this happened to a member of a large pilgrimage group.

He was dressed in a light suit without outer covering because he had lost his coat on the train from Paris the night before. Despite the cold and pouring rain, he wanted to attend Mass at the Grotto, so he decided to ignore both the rain and the cold.

About half an hour later, he wondered why he did not feel wet. He felt under his thin suit jacket. His undergarment was dry.

Incredulous. His first thought was that the suit, like a raincoat, was impermeable. Then he wondered why the pouring rain did not seem to be running down inside his collar.

"It's a funny kind of rain," he thought.

Next, he put his foot in a puddle on the esplanade, where the rainwater was coursing in flood. It went over the top of his shoe. Instinctively he bent to empty the water from the shoe only to find, to his amazement, that shoe, sock, and foot were dry.

At that moment, he realized he was experiencing a miracle.

What was happening? Had rain ceased to be rain? Had his clothes and himself suddenly become impermeable?

He and his clothes had not changed. The rain had not ceased to be rain. Other people around, to keep from getting wet, were wearing rain gear.

The only logical explanation is that the *wetting EFFECT* of the water *had been suspended* in relation to his person.

The Eucharistic Miracle

The theory accepted by many that all matter is made up of atoms, which in turn are made of counter points of force, casts light on what may be the nature of the great miracle of the Eucharist because, if all matter is made up of points of force, and if the EFFECT of those points of force were suspended in the body of a six foot man, weighing 180 pounds, *it would be possible for that body to fit on the pointed tip of a needle.*

The body would not cease to be a body just because the effects of the points of force were suspended. When that suspended force was restored, the body would be there, six feet tall and weighing 180 pounds.

If we presume that this is the nature of the great miracle of the Eucharist, explaining it does not diminish the greatness of the miracle, which also involves the suspension of the forces within the bread with which Our Lord becomes transubstantiated.

As in the case of St. Bernadette, although the candle did not burn her while she was seeing Our Lady, it would burn her afterwards. And while Our Lord is present under the accidents of bread (that is its extension, its whiteness, its taste) after transubstantiation, He is no longer there after the accidents change.

In Many Tabernacles

In addition to the Eucharistic miracle of transubstantiation, there is the wonder of the simultaneous presence of Our Lord in every Host, in every broken particle of every Host, and in every tabernacle of the world.

Light is cast on this wonder by considering the nature of a glorified body.

Jesus "materialized" before His apostles in a closed room. Had He come from somewhere through the wall? or down from the ceiling? or was He an apparition rather than really Jesus?

To prove that it was really Himself, He invited them to touch Him. He cast a shadow. He asked for food and ate with them. And when the visit was over, suddenly He was just not there.

Again, if matter is counter positioned points of force, could not Our Lord suspend the effect of that force whenever He wished, and restore it *whenever and wherever* He wished?

Obviously another quality of a resurrected body, at least certainly in the case of Our Lord, is to be *simultaneously in more than one place at the same time* because after His Resurrection, we know that while He was appearing in one place, He was also appearing in another. And always, it was wholly and completely the same Jesus.

Believing

In the case of the man in the rain at Lourdes, his first reaction was to seek a natural explanation: his clothes were waterproof, it was a "funny kind of rain."

But when his foot was submerged in a puddle and emerged dry, he suddenly realized it was a miracle. It was an act of *God*. And it was happening to him.

At that moment, he was like a person swimming for the first time in deep water and struck with fear, longing to be able touch bottom. It was too much. He cried out; "Lord, I believe, now let me get wet!"

But the Lord continued the miracle and the man not only made an act of faith, but like the swimmer who suddenly discovers that he can stay up as he swims, he rejoiced as he walked in the rain, praising God.

When he shared his experience with others (and in particular two members of his family who were on the same pilgrimage), even though they saw with their own eyes, they were incredulous. Although they nodded their heads, he could tell by looking into their eyes that their minds did not accept what they were seeing. For them, too, it had to be that the suit was impermeable or it was a "funny kind of rain."

Seeing is not always believing.

Act of Faith

What does it take to realize the wonder of the miracle of the Eucharist? What does it take to believe, really believe, that Our Lord becomes wholly and truly present within the accidents of bread when the priest repeats His words: "This is My Body."?

It takes an act of faith. It takes realization that this is *an act of God*. And even if one accepts the atomic concept of matter as points of force, and even if one understands that God can suspend the effect of any force in His creation, we must make that act of faith.

It would seem that comparatively few who "believe" in the Eucharist ever really make a complete act of faith. They believe because Our Lord said so, and the Church says so, but they do not fully grasp the reality of the great miracle that they profess to believe. They do not *realize* that Our Lord is wholly, truly, completely present in that little white Host, and in every Particle, and simultaneously in every tabernacle in the world.

If they did, would there ever be talking in church? Would we misuse the new options for receiving Him? Instead, how deeply we would genuflect and focus our attention on Him, truly present just as He became present in a closed room after His Resurrection!

How to Obtain this Faith

We are like the witnesses to the rain miracle at Lourdes who saw, believed what they saw, but did not believe in the miracle. They could not bridge the gap between the natural and the supernatural. What is more, since their minds said "impossible," they were not even tempted to try.

To believe in the miracle of the Eucharist, we must try.

First, we must realize that an act of faith in a miracle, which is the work of God, requires God's Grace. To swim in His deep water, without feeling the need of putting our feet on the ground of unbelief, we have to make the effort. We have to pray. Our Lady of Fatima is just waiting to bathe us in the light of Her Heart as she did for the children of Fatima. She was the world's first tabernacle. All of us, from Pope to peasant, receive the Eucharist from Her. She longs to have us know that He is truly present in the Blessed Sacrament.

The more we unite our hearts to Her Heart Immaculate, the more our faith and realization of the Eucharistic miracle will increase.

Our Lady of the Eucharist

This is the ultimate message of Fatima. We, too, like the three little children in the presence of the Angel can believe, adore, trust, and love. And in the light from Our Lady's Heart, we too can become "lost in God" and cry out with faith: "O Most Holy Trinity, I adore Thee! My God, My God, I love Thee in the Most Blessed Sacrament."

The promised triumph of the Immaculate Heart of Mary in the world will bring realization that Jesus is wholly and truly present in this Sacrament of Love.

We will then long for union with Her Immaculate Heart so that, as Our Lord told St. John Eudes, *we may have hearts worthy of Him.*

CHAPTER 21

Our Lady's Greatest Gift!

"Our Greatest Privilege from the Mother of God" –Pope Pius XI

W E HAVE ALREADY MENTIONED the Sabbatine Privilege is a great importance of motivation and the incentive for making and keeping the Blue Army pledge. Pope Pius XI called it **"Our greatest privilege from the Mother of God,** *extending even after death..."*

This privilege, first promulgated by Pope John XXII, has been ratified by many Popes. It promises *freedom from Purgatory soon after death,* especially on the First Saturday. It is specifically mentioned in the decree of Pope Pius X which, in giving permission for the Scapular Medal, says: *"Not excluding the Sabbatine Privilege."*

Satan abhors this greatest privilege from Our Heavenly Mother because it makes saints.

Saints Before We Die

St. Alphonsus, a Doctor of the Church, said we may hope *"not to go to Purgatory at all"* if we do a little more than the three simple conditions the privilege requires.

Pere Lamy said: "As for Our Lady, Her kindness gets Her everywhere... A soul that is falling into Hell and calls on Her is helped. *The Blessed Virgin said again to me one day that those who have fulfilled the conditions of Her Sabbatine Privilege will be drawn out of Purgatory by Her on the first Saturday after death."*

Our Lady told the Ven. Pere Lamy that few obtain this great privilege *because few fulfill the conditions.*

Our Lady has now made the conditions of the Sabbatine Privilege easily available to all in the Blue Army pledge.

Final Vision of Fatima

Asked why Our Lady held the Scapular from the sky in the final vision of Fatima, Sister Lucia said this is because *"She wishes everyone to wear it; it is the sign of consecration to Her Immaculate Heart."*

This consecration, which is at the heart of the Fatima message, *is the key to obtaining this privilege*. It is the magic key to the door of holiness. And the Sabbatine Privilege *is a great incentive to use that key in our daily lives.*

Indeed, how foolish we would be if we were to hesitate even for one moment to put ourselves beneath Our Lady's mantle by being enrolled in Her Scapular! And how foolish again if we would fail to fulfill the other two simple conditions of Her

Sabbatine Privilege—*"the greatest of all our privileges from the Mother of God, extending even after death."*

The Three Conditions

In 1324, when this "super indulgence" was first promulgated, the conditions were three:

1) Chastity according to one's state of life;

2) The Scapular;

3) The Little Office of the Blessed Virgin or, if one could not read, fasting on Wednesdays and Fridays.

All priests have the faculty to enroll in the Scapular included in their diocesan faculties. This includes the faculty to commute the third condition to some other prayer or work.

In 1950, the Blue Army of Our Lady of Fatima obtained permission from the Prior General of the Carmelite Order to substitute the Rosary for the third condition. A request was then included on the Blue Army membership pledge to substitute the Rosary for the third condition for all its members.[83] The Blue Army pledge fulfilled the three conditions for the Privilege.

The First Condition

The first and most important condition is the observance of chastity according to our state in life. This is also the first and most important condition for response to the message of Fatima: "Men must stop offending God Who is already too much offended."

---

[83] A note is usually appended to the Blue Amy pledge with a box to be checked because each person, on joining the Blue Army, must make the request. This is required because the Rosary is not the only possible substitution.

Blessed Jacinta, informed by Our Lady of Fatima, said: "*Most souls go to Hell because of sins of impurity.*" Although many such sins are committed mostly from human weakness, many souls are lost because of *failure to confess these sins and to make a firm resolution to avoid them.*

Committing sins against impurity does not deprive us of the Sabbatine Privilege. *Only failure to confess,* and lack of a sincere intention of remaining chaste, can deprive us of this "greatest of all privileges from the Mother of God." And, in the very conditions for this privilege, Our Lady helps us.

The Wonder of the Fatima Pledge

Being a practical mother, Our Lady placed the primary condition of avoiding sin in a positive form. She requests *the sanctification of our daily duties.*

She asks us to *offer them up*, in reparation for our sins and those of the world. This is done quite simply by making *the Morning Offering* and extending it through the day with the two aids She offers: *The Scapular and the Rosary.*

She had already been encouraging us along this simple path of holiness for almost seven hundred years through the Sabbatine Privilege. Now, She tells us at Fatima that this is not only a path to our personal holiness but also a path to the triumph of Her Immaculate Heart in the entire world.

She invites us to enter into the light of Her Immaculate Heart which prevents the flaming sword of the Angel of God's Justice from striking the world with fire. She invites us to join the special cohort of saints, the power of whose prayer, in union with Her Heart, will turn back the tidal wave of evil.

These three simple conditions offer us the assurance that we shall be saints *before we die*. Indeed, how else could we be freed from Purgatory by the first Saturday after death *if we had not by then become holy?*

As mentioned above, St. Alphonsus, Doctor of the Church, went so far as to say that if we do **a little more** than what is required for the Sabbatine Privilege, **"may we not hope that we will not go to Purgatory AT ALL?"** And forty years after the death of the saint, his brown Scapular was found perfectly preserved midst the corruption of all else corruptible in his tomb.

We recall again that Pere Lamy, who saw the coming triumph of the Immaculate Heart of Mary, said: "As for Our Lady, Her kindness gets Her everywhere... A soul that is falling into Hell and calls on Her is helped. *The Blessed Virgin said again to me one day that those who have fulfilled the conditions of Her Sabbatine Privilege will be drawn out of Purgatory by Her on the first Saturday after death."*[84]

How Precious!

This was said in 1924, not long after Pope Saint Pius X had given permission for the use of the Scapular medal adding, in the papal decree, *"not excluding the Sabbatine Privilege."* The Pope gave this permission for serious reasons, such as conditions in the trenches during the First World War. Pere Lamy said:

---

[84] *Pere Lamy, Apostle and Mystic,* by Paul Biver, pg. 85. See also *Pere Lamy,* by the same author, published 1973 by TAN, pgs. 67 and 95.

"How precious then is the Brown Scapular which brings us deliverance from such places of pain, for Purgatory is extremely painful. The Blessed Virgin told me that She thought it better to stay behind 15 years, dragging one's weight on earth, than to spend 15 minutes in Purgatory."

Also, how precious is the virtue of chastity!— the one virtue which is the prime condition for obtaining this great Privilege.

The Second Condition, the Rosary

Venerable Pere Lamy saw Our Lady with the Rosary in front of Her Immaculate Heart. He said: "This devotion *goes to Her Heart.* How She loves, through this devotion, to shed Her blessings on the earth!"

Today the Rosary is so needed to turn back the tidal wave of impurity that *Our Lady asked for it in each and every one of Her Fatima apparitions.*

In addition, She asked for fifteen minutes of meditation on the mysteries of the Rosary on the First Saturday of every month.

She also asked that on this day, we confess our sins and receive Holy Communion, offering all in reparation for the sins committed against Her Most Pure Heart.

We may rejoice that it was made so easy for the Rosary to be substituted for the Little Office for the majority of Catholics, as was done with the little box at the bottom of the Blue Army pledge.[85]

---

[85] For further information, see the author's booklet *All You Need to Know about the Scapular*, available from the 101 Foundation.

The Third Condition, the Scapular

The third condition for the Sabbatine Privilege is the Scapular of Mount Carmel. One of the strongest motives for wearing this Scapular (with an understanding that it is an act of faith, hope and love and of consecration to the Immaculate Heart of Mary) is that *it is a great aid and safeguard for the beautiful virtue of purity, especially when combined with the Rosary.*

Indeed, it has been said: "No one can wear the Scapular and say the fifteen decades of the Rosary daily with attention to the mysteries and remain in mortal sin."[86]

After Sister Lucia said: "She (Our Lady) wishes everyone to wear it; it is the sign of consecration to Her Immaculate Heart," she was asked if therefore the Scapular was necessary for fulfillment of the requests of Our Lady of Fatima.

Sister Lucia replied that it was.

She added that she felt Our Lady did not say this in so many words *"because it was understood"* by Our Lady holding out the Scapular in the final vision after insisting over and over on consecration to Her Immaculate Heart.

"As Pope Pius XII," has said, Sister Lucia pointed out, "the Scapular is our sign of consecration to the Immaculate Heart of Mary... The Scapular and the Rosary are inseparable."

She said further that she believes that *if she had not understood this*, Our Lady would have spoken of it.[87]

---

[86] See the author's book *Sex and the Mysteries*, published by the 101 Foundation.

Power of the Scapular

As mentioned above, Blessed Jacinta reported that Our Lady said: *"Most souls go to Hell because of sins of the flesh."*

Conversely, we may say that most chaste souls go to Heaven. And souls are chaste when there is a *sincere intention* to be chaste.

The faithful wearing of the Scapular is a sign of that intention.

Let it be said again that the condition of the Sabbatine Privilege (that we observe chastity according to our state of life) does not mean that if we commit a sin against chastity we will lose the privilege. If we are in the state of Grace and *have a sincere intention not to sin,* we are fulfilling the Sabbatine condition.

The power of the Scapular and Rosary is to keep us in that sincere intention.

By the Scapular, we are consecrated to the Immaculate Heart of Mary. As we wear it, the strings over our shoulders are like Our Lady's arms protecting us. The panel over our hearts symbolizes being beneath Her powerfully protecting mantle. Ven. Francis Yepes, brother of St. John of the Cross, said that the Scapular is one of the three things most dreaded by Satan because it is "the sign" of the Immaculate! When we pray the Rosary with awareness of this, we drive evil away.

---

[87] From interview with V. Rev. Howard Rafferty, O.Carm. When asked about the accuracy of these statements, a few months before his death, Father Howard said he was "absolutely certain," and referred to the recording he made at the time.

To those who wear the Scapular and say the Rosary devoutly, sins against chastity become abhorrent. And if we should be snared by them, we will fly to Confession. Thus we become saints, rejoicing in those words of the great Marian Doctor, Saint Alphonsus Liguori:

"And if we do a little more than Our Lady asks, can we not hope that we will not go to Purgatory at all?"

Is not a "little more" the devotion of the five First Saturdays?[88] These, too, remind us of this great privilege, which is often called simply: The First Saturday Privilege.[89]

The two-hundred-year-old scapular of St. Alphonsus shows it to be remarkable even had it not been in the tomb for forty years. The cotton picture is even intact, with the thread fastening it to the wool. Yet in the tomb, all beneath and above it turned to dust. It was found as pictured here... on the saint's skeleton. Examination proves that it had no special treatment that could account for this wonder.

---

[88] In an interview of October 11, 1993, Sister Lucia said Our Lady wants all the conditions of the pledge but that especially now, in what she called the "post-consecration phase" of Fatima, Our Lady asks for the devotion of the Five First Saturdays. See *Duas Entrevistas com a Irma Lucia* published at Fatima by Regina Press, May 1998.

[89] References for the quotations in this chapter can be found in the author's book *Sign of Her Heart*, published by the 101 Foundation.

CHAPTER 22

Leap from the Past

The last century began to sift good
from bad. It gave us the Second Vatican
Council, springboard to the New Era.

W E HAVE SPOKEN about work still to be
done and challenges to the future, with
only brief reference to the radical
changes in the Church experienced in the last
century.

Soon the new generation will no longer be distracted by the changes. We tend to forget when
tempests are over, preoccupied as we are with the
present and the future.

There were also tempests in the nineteenth century, at the end of which my parents were born. They
spoke little about those trials perhaps because they
were so taken up by the changes taking place in
the exciting century which followed.

They did not think to speak about the immi-
grant struggles to adapt to a new land, or life in
towns with horse-drawn trolleys and dirt roads, or

even of the devastating Civil War which almost threatened the end of the United States of America as we know it.

I lived all but fifteen years of the twentieth century. My impressions of the previous century in which my parents were born came from seeing Civil War veterans marching on the Fourth of July and seeing horse-drawn vehicles gradually replaced by those driven by steam and gasoline.

Changes from the dawn of the twentieth century to its end were constantly amazing.

The twenty-first century, opening the new millennium with even more rapid changes of technology, is likely soon to forget the century past. But it cannot forget that the fulfillment of the message of Fatima is the primary burden of this new century. At its dawn, Sister Lucia, who on May 13, 2000, attended the beatification of the companions who received the message with her, said that now:

"Fatima is in its third day...the triumph is an ongoing process."

The Great Change

To me, great heroes of the twentieth century were persons like Chesterton, Frank Sheed, Belloc, the Popes (all of them!), Father Daniel Lord, Father Peyton, Dorothy Day, Archbishop Sheen, Mother Teresa—most of whom I had personally met. It was a century of a host of brilliant defenders of faith and morality. Catholics who were told the message of Fatima gradually accepted it, especially after 1942 when Pope Pius XII made the first act of the consecration of the world to the Immaculate Heart. But the world in general ignored this heavenly intervention, the most important event of the century.[90]

Then came the 1960's. Amazing changes in the ensuing years were not of new discoveries but the denigration of old values.

As we were just becoming aware of the changes which had begun to convulse the world, Pope John XXIII stunned the Church with the announcement of the Council.

I took an apartment in Rome during the Council, primarily with the intention of being close to the Bishop of Fatima and promoting the Collegial Consecration. I witnessed this transforming event of the twentieth century as few other laymen were privileged to do.

The West, which had been secularized by war and by the spread of militant atheism from Russia throughout the world, had begun to succumb to secularism. As Gian Franco Svidercoschi said: "Modern 'progress' was leaving a long trail of ambiguities, doubts, fears."[91] Vatican II became the object of diverging interpretations.

The Tempest

These eventually degenerated into two increasingly antithetical tendencies. Excesses on one side led to excesses on the other.

In fear, many of the devout polarized in tradition. They absolutized the past. They resisted the

---

[90] See the author's book *God's Final Effort*, available from the 101 Foundation.

[91] Author of *History of the Council*, and confidante of Pope John Paul II. Many of the thoughts expressed here were inspired by his article *The Crisis of '68* in *Inside the Vatican*, February 2000.

smallest changes in their Christian life. Minor schisms resulted, such as the sects of Sede Vacante and Marcel Lefebvre.

On the other side, all traditional values were questioned. Dogmas of the faith were brought into question. Hans Kung, who had come to be respected as an outstanding theologian, unexpectedly attacked even the dogma of papal infallibility. Apostasy reared its head.

"An anarchic wind blew like a tempest into the seminaries, the monasteries, and the parishes. A large number of priests deserted, and an even larger number of women religious. Some convents were left almost empty. Vocations collapsed. There were violent press campaigns against the encyclical *Humanae Vitae* and against priestly celibacy."[92]

Pope Paul VI had delayed six years before issuing *Humane Vitae*. Svidercoschi says the Pope was living "an hour of uncertainty, of self-criticism, and even of self destruction." He seemed restrained, even imprisoned, by the tempest which was shaking the Church. As I mentioned in a previous book, I will never forget the Pope's expression when, at the end of an interview, he turned back and said to me: *"Pray for me. Pray for me."*

New Century Will Benefit

But what would have happened to the Church were it not for the Council? The new century will reap the benefits of its definition of doctrine and especially of its innovative teaching on the role of the laity in the life of the Church. As I said in *You, Too!*, this is the great leap forward from the past.

---

[92] Ibid.

"It was thanks to the Council," says Svidercoschi, "that in the end, Catholicism emerged from the crisis. Thanks to the Council, but also to Pope Paul VI, who was at the center of the storm. He was disobeyed, debated, even insulted. And yet, he was able to defend the Creed, the moral law, the dignity of the human person, and thus restore unity and prophecy to the Church. Paul VI was an authentic reformer precisely because he never saw Vatican II as an end, but as a beginning."

Those of the new century may know little of the tempest. But they will have to adjust and work around the debris it left behind.

The Leap

How will God fill the vacuum left by the priests who, in the tempest and collapse of morality, deserted? How will He fill the vacuum of decimated religious communities? How will those who have survived the tempest restore the Church? Pope John Paul II said that he knew the victory will come through Mary. And he wrote a book-length apostolic letter calling for the involvement of the laity. He set the example of total consecration to Mary.

The first message of Fatima was that "God wishes to establish in the world devotion to the Immaculate Heart of Mary." Scarcely grasped in the last century, this is the greatest challenge to the new.

Far from God after the bloodiest century in history, which was accented by worldwide militant atheism, the new century will find God-Father in the human being through whom He sent His Son. It will find the Holy Spirit in the human being to whom He became the Spouse to give us a Savior. It will find Jesus, Who came to us through Her.

Like the children of Fatima, *in the light streaming from Her Heart*, we will be *"lost in God"* and exclaim: *"O Most Holy Trinity! I adore Thee! My God, my God, I love Thee in the Most Blessed Sacrament."*

The leap from the past will be a leap of faith and confidence in the message and promise of Fatima in which all the faithful are called to be involved.

Sent by God, Our Lady foretold the tempest in 1917. There would be another war *worse than the war (which America had entered that same year) "to end all wars."* The good would be persecuted. The Pope would suffer. Errors of atheism would engulf the world.

BUT, if Her requests are heard, there will be a complete turnaround. The tempest will be over. Her Immaculate Heart will triumph. A glorious era of faith will follow.

The new century does not seem sufficiently aware of that promise. It does not seem to realize that, by a solemn promise from Heaven, confirmed during Vatican Council II at the solemn moment of the promulgation of *Lumen Gentium*, if the requests of Our Lady of Fatima are heard, *there will be a complete turnaround.*

Before All Bishops of the World

Many seem to think the Fatima Apostolate is, as Carl Malburg put it, "an underground movement or, at best, a fringe group of Catholics."[93] Yet in the most solemn moment of the Council, when the major document on the Church was promulgated, in the presence of all the bishops of the world, Pope Paul VI said:

> "Meditation on the close relationships between Mary and the Church, so clearly established

In this intimate apparition, Our Lord said: "Behold the Heart of your Most Holy Mother covered with thorns..." Our Lady asked for Communions of Reparation on five consecutive First Saturdays.

in today's conciliar Constitution *Lumen Gentium*, makes us feel this is the most solemn and appropriate moment to fulfill a wish which we made at the end of the preceding session (of the Council), and which very many Council Fathers have made their own... *We proclaim the Most Blessed Virgin Mary Mother of the Church.*

"We trust then, with the promulgation of The Constitution on the Church *sealed by proclamation of Mary as Mother of the Church*...the Christian people may turn to the Holy Virgin.

"Our venerated predecessor, Pius XII, not without pious inspiration, solemnly consecrated (the world) to the Immaculate Heart of Mary. Today we consider it particularly appropriate to recall this act of consecration. With this in mind, we have decided to send a special mission to Fatima... In this manner, *we intend to entrust to the care of this heavenly Mother the entire human family*, with its problems and anxieties, with its legitimate aspirations and ardent hopes."

Although the Pope said that many bishops shared his thought, he knew many did not. Many felt that such "extreme" affirmation of the role of Mary to fulfill the world's "ardent hopes" might be a detriment to ecumenism. Therefore, at the end of this most important declaration to the world's bishops, the Pope added:

---

[93] Carl Malburg, custodian of the International Pilgrim Virgin Statue, is a fulltime Fatima apostle with international experience. He was a member of the national executive committee of the Blue Army before becoming custodian, and for more than ten years has traveled and lectured on the message of Fatima in parishes in North and South America, in Asia, and in Europe.

"Above all, we desire that it should be made clear that Mary, the Humble Handmaid of the Lord, exists only in relation to God and to Christ, our sole Mediator and Redeemer. *May the true nature and the aims of Marian veneration in the Church be made clear, particularly where there are many separated brothers, so that all those who are not part of the Catholic community may understand that devotion to Mary*, far from being an end in itself, is instead a means *essentially ordained to orient souls to Christ* and thus unite them with the Father in the love of the Holy Spirit."

Make Her Role CLEAR!

The more we know about the message of Fatima and its affirmation by the Church, the more we realize that it is a Divine intervention at a most critical moment in history.

The above quotations from the declaration of the Pope, *"sealing" the promulgation of the major Council document*, were deliberately made *"at this most solemn and appropriate moment."*

This was not the message just of an apparition to three children on the far western end of Europe. This was a solemn declaration, at a most solemn moment, in the presence of ALL THE BISHOPS OF THE WORLD.

And its impact on the new century is yet to be grasped.

"Above all," the Pope said, the relationship of Mary to Jesus "should be made clear...particularly where there are many separated brothers, so that ALL (emphasis added) may understand that devotion to Mary...is essentially ordained to orient souls to Christ AND THUS UNITE THEM with the Father in the love of the Holy Spirit."

Islam

The greatest obstacle to the world's "ardent hopes" for the "era of peace for mankind" is religious division and especially of confrontation with Islam. The latter could be the flash point of atomic destruction.

It is an "obstacle" *essentially connected with Fatima and the Fatima Apostolate.*

"God wishes to establish in the world devotion to the Immaculate Heart of Mary." And She chose to be known by the name of Mohammed's daughter of whom the Prophet of Islam said: "Fatima (his daughter) has the highest place in Heaven *after the Virgin Mary.*" And **these words are in the Koran, the holy book of Islam.**

Though some see Marian devotion as a stumbling block to ecumenism, it is the key.

This was perhaps the most important message of Kibeho as Father Gabriel Maindron remarks: "The Virgin never asked the Protestants or Muslims to be converted or to become Catholics, but to recognize Her as Mother of God and, in this recognition, pray to Her."[94]

As for the different religions, Our Lady said at Kibeho, Rwanda (before crowds which included persons of many religions): "Do not be disturbed. All are children of God. Before God, there are not Protestants, Catholics, Adventists, Muslims, and so on... The Mother of God wants you to know that *before God, we are all children of God. The true child of God is the one who does the Will of God. God*

---

[94] See the author's books, *Too Late?* and *God's Final Effort*, both available from the 101 Foundation.

regards the love you have for Him and for your neighbor."

This does not mean that all religions are equal. It means that those who live according to their conscience are pleasing to God. It means that *if all turn to Our Lady in prayer, She will show Herself a Mother to all.* She will lead all to unity in Jesus.

The Challenge

We have written of the Muslims with relation to Our Lady at length in other books and will not go into it further here. In essence: if we do as Our Lady of Fatima asks, the obstacle of religious confrontation will be overcome. Her Heart, Her Motherly love, will triumph.

Those who have survived the spiritual and moral tempest of the last century must now take the leap of faith as did the Blessed Children of Fatima. The challenge to the new century is to reach out to *the entire world*, as Cardinal Tisserant said, with the "specific response." They are challenged to "make clear," as Paul VI said as he promulgated *Lumen Gentium* (Light to the Nations), that Mary is the Mother of the Savior to Whom God has now entrusted the peace of the world.

The new generation is challenged to explain what we mean by the titles "Co-Redemptrix, Mediatrix, and Advocate." It is challenged to explain that, as the new Eve, She is *the spiritual Mother of every person on the earth*, and everyone, of every nation and class, can trust in Her promise: "If you do as I ask, many souls will be saved... *An era of peace will be granted to mankind.*"

The "Blue Army," in its broad sense, is the spiritual army of ALL who commit themselves to the specific response given at Fatima. *No one has to be*

part of its "organization." The Blue Army organization is *for those who want to be apostles* for the
triumph as part of the official, Church-authorized
Fatima Apostolate.

What is important is the spiritual response
which Sister Lucia formulated into a pledge and
which a pious parish priest asked his parishioners
to witness with a sign of blue as members of a
spiritual army consecrated to Her Immaculate
Heart.

The Legacy

I hope in these pages, we have indicated, in
some small way, part of the legacy of the past
century and *the urgency* of following through before it is too late. It is the legacy of the bloodiest
century in history. The challenge of that century,
to those who follow, *is to place trust in the great
promise made in 1917,* which was confirmed by a
miracle "so that all may believe."

It is the legacy of giving to the world, as Pope
John Paul II said, "the specific response to save man
from self-destruction." It is the legacy of a century
of war-fulfilled prophecies, holding forth the final
choice of triumph by Grace rather than by fire.

From this legacy, there emerges the "new and
divine holiness" of those totally consecrated to Mary.

Redemption triumphed completely in Her. With
Her and by Her, redemption can triumph in us. We
can live in the Divine Will with a power that will
change the face of the earth.

New Power

As we mentioned earlier, Saint Faustina who
reached this level of the new and divine holiness,
dared one day to ask Our Lord that ALL who died

that day would be saved. *And Jesus granted Her request.*

It was a Friday. She had been praying all day for dying sinners. But she hesitated to make so great a request. Then Jesus encouraged her: "What is it that you desire to tell me?"

"Jesus, I beg You," the saint finally dared to say, "that all the souls who die today escape the fire of Hell, even if they have been the greatest sinners. Today is Friday,[95] the day of your Agony. Because Your Mercy is inconceivable, the angels will not be surprised at this."

Our Lord replied: *"You have come to know well the depths of My Mercy. I will do what you ask. But unite yourself continually to My agonizing Heart and make reparation to My Justice. Know that you have asked Me for a great thing..."* (873).

Great indeed! Oh, the power of the prayer of this one saint in the new and divine holiness! Life would have had to be prolonged on that day for those souls who refused the Grace offered, but thus giving even to them the Mercy of more time to be saved.

A Daring Prayer

"Lead ALL souls to Heaven," is the prayer Our Lady taught us to say at the end of each decade of the Rosary. Would She have taught us a prayer which could not be answered?

There will be great spiritual power in the totus tuus saints (like Saint Faustina) *in the new era.*

Perhaps obdurate sinners, who sin against the Holy Spirit Himself, will have to be removed before the time of triumph. Perhaps they will remain

---

[95] It was January 8, 1937.

like weeds with the grain to be separated at the end and burned.

We do not know how it will all happen. But we know that the Immaculate Heart of Mary will triumph with the Eucharistic Heart of Jesus.

Enough *totus tuus* souls can make it possible without the terrible chastisement which "so far," Our Lady has been holding back because of just a few.

The journey to the triumph begins with the "specific response": the Blue Army pledge. It soars to perfection in total consecration.

Deadline

We would like to conclude with the same words that will be used at the end of the sequel to this book, which will be titled *To Shake the World.*

In the final apparition of October 13, 1917, Our Lady identified Herself as "Our Lady of the Rosary," performing a great miracle "so that all may believe."

In Her first words of the July apparition (the apparition of the Secret), She said we must pray the Rosary for peace *"in honor of Our Lady of the Rosary, because only She can help you."*

We deserve God's Justice, but in His Mercy, He empowers Her to help us now with one condition: That we assist Her with our response.

To understand this is to understand the urgency of the Fatima Apostolate. We find excellent examples in Scripture.

Only She Can Help

In the Old Testament, we have the example of Satan challenging God that *he could destroy Job and cause him to blaspheme* if God did not assist him. God said to Satan, "Do what thou wilt," giving time for the test.

We are told that at the beginning of the last century Satan gave a similar challenge to God: "Give me a hundred years and I will bring mankind to self-destruction." We are told that God granted Satan the hundred years, because of which Pope Leo XIII mandated a prayer to Saint Michael after every Mass. He also wrote 18 exhortations/encyclicals on the Rosary!

Satan has had his time during the bloodiest century in history. Our Lady of the Rosary, destined to crush his head, now comes to the world in great power under the sign of "the greatest, most colossal miracle in history."

She calls upon Her children to help Her as holy followers of Moses once helped him in his prayer for victory against the forces of Amalec.

Holding up the Arms of Moses

When the battle was going badly for the Israelites, Moses prayed with outstretched arms. As long as he did so, the battle went in the favor of God's people. When Moses could no longer hold out his arms, the battle favored the forces of Amalec.

So, the holy followers of Moses *held up his arms until the victory was won.*

This is what we must do for Our Lady to whom, as Blessed Jacinta said, God has now *"entrusted the peace of the world"*...as He once entrusted the victory of God's people to Moses.

Needed now are a sufficient number to respond to that call. Saint Padre Pio indicated this when he said: "Russia will be converted when there is a Blue Army member for every Communist."

This modern holy man and prophet was saying: "The victory will come *when there are a sufficient number of souls* responding to Our Lady's requests."

This writer was present (together with Cardinal Stritch, Msgr. Colgan, and a small group of priests) when Saint Padre Pio said this. Hardly believing my ears, I asked what he had said. He firmly repeated the same statement in exactly the same words.

Now, in the light of the revelation of the final Secret of Fatima, that need of a *sufficient number* is reaching a deadline. The Vatican document, revealing the Secret on June 26, 2000, is startlingly clear:

"The Angel with the flaming sword recalls similar images in the Book of Revelation. *This represents the threat of judgment over the world.* Today, the prospect that the world might be *reduced to ashes by a sea of fire* is no longer pure fantasy. *Man himself, with his inventions, has forged the flaming sword."*

Will we obtain the sufficient number in time to prevent that flaming sword from striking us?

AFTERWORD

From Jesus

TO BLESSED Dina Belanger:

"No invocation responds better to the immense desire of My Eucharistic Heart to reign in souls than: *Eucharistic Heart of Jesus, may Your Kingdom come through the Immaculate Heart of Mary.*"

To Saint Faustina:

"It is with pleasure that I look into your soul. I bestow many Graces only because of you. I also withhold My punishments because of you. You restrain Me, and I cannot vindicate the claims of My Justice. You bind My Hands with your love (1193).

"In the Old Covenant, I sent prophets wielding thunderbolts to My people. Today I am sending you with My Mercy to the people of the whole world. I *do not want to punish aching mankind. Instead, I desire to heal it, pressing it to My Merciful Heart.*

"I use punishment when they themselves force Me to do so. My Hand is reluctant to take hold of the sword of Justice. Before the Day of Justice I am sending the Day of My Mercy" (1588).

"When in Heaven you see these present days, you will rejoice and will want to see as many of them as possible" (1787).

Following is a description of a vision given to Saint Faustina of the impending chastisement and of the power God deigned to give to her prayer. It was perhaps this to which Jesus referred when He said that when the saint was in Heaven she would rejoice to see "these present days" she was then living, days in which she was gaining Graces for the entire world. She writes:

"I saw an Angel, the executor of Divine Wrath. He was clothed in dazzling robe, his face gloriously bright, a cloud beneath his feet. From the cloud, bolts of thunder and flashes of lightning were springing into his hands and from his hands they were going forth, and only then were they striking the earth.

"When I saw this sign of Divine Wrath which was about to strike the earth... I began to implore the Angel to hold off for a few moments, and the world would do penance.

"But my plea was a mere nothing in the Face of the Divine Anger.

"Just then I saw the Most Holy Trinity. The greatness of Its Majesty pierced me deeply and I did not dare to repeat my entreaties. Then, at that very moment, I felt in my soul the power of Jesus' Grace, which dwells in my soul. When I became conscious of this Grace I was instantly snatched up before the Throne of God. Oh, how great is Our Lord and God and how incomprehensible His Holiness! I found myself pleading for the world with words heard interiorly.

"As I was praying in this manner, I saw the Angel's helplessness. *He could not carry out the just punishment which was rightly due for sins.*

Never before had I prayed with such inner power as then" (474).

Jesus said to her that her "smallest act" was now of *"infinite value."* He added:

"A pure soul has *inconceivable power* before God" (534).

The Fatima pledge opens the door to this power. The total consecration takes us through the door of the Immaculate Heart of Mary, the Mother of Mercy, to whom God has now entrusted the peace of the world. On the other side of the door is the triumph of the Sacred Hearts in the "new and divine holiness."

"WOMAN, BEHOLD YOUR SON!"

244

Act of Entrustment to Mary Most Holy
Pope John Paul II, October 8, 2000

1. "WOMAN, BEHOLD YOUR SON!" (Jn 19:26). As we near the end of this Jubilee Year, when you, O Mother, have offered us Jesus anew, the blessed fruit of your womb most pure, the Word made flesh, the world's Redeemer, we hear more clearly the sweet echo of His words entrusting us to you, making you our Mother: "Woman, behold your son!" When He entrusted to you the Apostle John, and with him the children of the Church and all people, Christ did not diminish but affirmed anew the role which is His alone as the Savior of the world. You are the splendor which in no way dims the light of Christ, for you exist in Him and through Him. Everything in you is fiat: you are the Immaculate One, through you there shines the fullness of Grace. Here, then, are your children gathered before you at the dawn of the new Millennium. The Church today, through the voice of the Successor of Peter, in union with so many Pastors assembled here from every corner of the world, seeks refuge in your motherly protection and trustingly begs your intercession as she faces the challenges which lie hidden in the future.

2. In this year of Grace, countless people have known the overflowing joy of the Mercy which the Father has given us in Christ. In the particular Churches throughout the world, and still more in this center of Christianity, the widest array of people have accepted this gift. Here the enthusiasm of the young rang out, here the sick have lifted

up their prayer. Here have gathered priests and religious, artists and journalists, workers and people of learning, children and adults, and all have acknowledged in your beloved Son the Word of God made flesh in your womb. O Mother, intercede for us, that the fruits of this Year will not be lost and that the seeds of Grace will grow to the full measure of the holiness to which we are all called.

We can turn this world into a garden,

or reduce it to a pile of rubble.

3. Today we wish to entrust to you the future that awaits us, and we ask you to be with us on our way. We are the men and women of an extraordinary time, exhilarating yet full of contradictions. Humanity now has instruments of unprecedented power: we can turn this world into a garden, or reduce it to a pile of rubble. We have devised the astounding capacity to intervene in the very well–springs of life: man can use this power for good, within the bounds of the moral law, or he can succumb to the short–sighted pride of a science which accepts no limits, but tramples on the respect due to every human being. Today as never before in the past, humanity stands at a crossroads. And once again, O Virgin Most Holy, salvation lies fully and uniquely in Jesus, your Son.

4. Therefore, O Mother, like the Apostle John, we wish to take you into our home (cf. Jn 19:27), that we may learn from you to become like your Son. "Woman, behold your son!" Here we stand before you to entrust to your maternal care ourselves, the Church, the entire world. Plead for us with your beloved Son that he may give us in abundance the Holy Spirit, the Spirit of truth which is the fountain of life. Receive the Spirit for us and with us, as happened in the first community gathered round you in Jerusalem on the day of Pentecost (cf. Acts 1:14). May the Spirit open our hearts to justice and love, and guide people and nations to mutual understanding and a firm desire for peace. We entrust to you all people, beginning with the weakest: the babies yet unborn, and those born into poverty and suffering, the young in search of meaning, the unemployed, and those suffering hunger and disease. We entrust to you all troubled families, the elderly with no one to help them, and all who are alone and without hope.

5. O Mother, you know the sufferings and hopes of the Church and the world: come to the aid of your children in the daily trials which life brings to each one, and grant that, thanks to the efforts of all, the darkness will not prevail over the light. To you, Dawn of Salvation, we commit our journey through the new Millennium, so that with you as guide all people may know Christ, the Light of the world and its only Savior, Who reigns with the Father and the Holy Spirit for ever and ever. Amen.

APPENDIX 2

Congregation for the
Doctrine of the Faith
The Message of Fatima
Introduction

A S THE SECOND MILLENNIUM gives way to the third,
Pope John Paul II has decided to publish the text
of the third part of the "Secret of Fatima."

The twentieth century was one of the most crucial in
human history, with its tragic and cruel events culminating in the assassination attempt on the "sweet Christ on
earth." Now a veil is drawn back on a series of events which
make history and interpret it in depth, in a spiritual per-
spective alien to present-day attitudes, often tainted with
rationalism.

Throughout history there have been supernatural apparitions and signs which go to the heart of human events
and which, to the surprise of believers and nonbelievers
alike, play their part in the unfolding of history. These
manifestations can never contradict the content of faith,
and must therefore have their focus in the core of Christ's
proclamation: the Father's love which leads men and women
to conversion and bestows the Grace required to abandon
oneself to Him with filial devotion. This too is the message of Fatima which, with its urgent call to conversion
and penance, draws us to the heart of the Gospel.

Fatima is undoubtedly the most prophetic of modern
apparitions. The first and second parts of the "Secret"—
which are here published in sequence so as to complete

the documentation—refer especially to the frightening vision of Hell, devotion to the Immaculate Heart of Mary, the Second World War, and finally the prediction of the immense damage that Russia would do to humanity by abandoning the Christian faith and embracing Communist totalitarianism.

In 1917 no one could have imagined all this: the three pastorinhos of Fatima see, listen and remember, and Lucia, the surviving witness, commits it all to paper when ordered to do so by the Bishop of Leiria and with Our Lady's permission.

For the account of the first two parts of the "Secret," which have already been published and are therefore known, we have chosen the text written by Sister Lucia in the Third Memoir of 31 August 1941; some annotations were added in the Fourth Memoir of 8 December 1941.

The third part of the "Secret" was written "by order of His Excellency the Bishop of Leiria and the Most Holy Mother..." on 3 January 1944.

There is only one manuscript, which is here reproduced photostatically. The sealed envelope was initially in the custody of the Bishop of Leiria. To ensure better protection for the "Secret" the envelope was placed in the Secret Archives of the Holy Office on 4 April 1957. The Bishop of Leiria informed Sister Lucia of this.

According to the records of the Archives, the Commissary of the Holy Office, Father Pierre Paul Philippe, OP, with the agreement of Cardinal Alfredo Ottaviani, brought the envelope containing the third part of the "Secret of Fatima" to Pope John XXIII on 17 August 1959. "After some hesitation," His Holiness said: "We shall wait. I shall pray. I shall let you know what I decide."[1]

In fact, Pope John XXIII decided to return the sealed envelope to the Holy Office and not to reveal the third part of the "Secret."

---

[1] From the diary of John XXIII, 17 August 1959: "Audiences: Father Philippe, Commissary of the Holy Office, who brought me the letter containing the third part of the Secrets of Fatima. I intend to read it with my Confessor."

Paul VI read the contents with the Substitute, Archbishop Angelo Dell'Acqua, on 27 March 1965, and returned the envelope to the Archives of the Holy Office, deciding not to publish the text.

John Paul II, for his part, asked for the envelope containing the third part of the "Secret" following the assassination attempt on 13 May 1981. On 18 July 1981 Cardinal Franjo Seper, Prefect of the Congregation, gave two envelopes to Archbishop Eduardo Martínez Somalo, Substitute of the Secretariat of State: one white envelope, containing Sister Lucia's original text in Portuguese; the other orange, with the Italian translation of the "Secret." On the following 11 August, Archbishop Martínez returned the two envelopes to the Archives of the Holy Office.[2]

As is well known, Pope John Paul II immediately thought of consecrating the world to the Immaculate Heart of Mary and he himself composed a prayer for what he called an "Act of Entrustment," which was to be celebrated in the Basilica of Saint Mary Major on 7 June 1981, the Solemnity of Pentecost, the day chosen to commemorate the 1600th anniversary of the First Council of Constantinople and the 1550th anniversary of the Council of Ephesus. Since the Pope was unable to be present, his recorded Address was broadcast. The following is the part which refers specifically to the Act of Entrustment:

That Convulse the World

"*Mother of all individuals and peoples*, you know all their sufferings and hopes. In your motherly heart you feel all the struggles between good and evil, between light and darkness, that convulse the world: accept the plea which we make in the Holy Spirit directly to your heart, and *embrace with the love of the Mother and Handmaid of the Lord those who most await this embrace*, and **also those whose act of entrustment you too await in a particular way**. Take under your motherly protection the whole

---

[2] The Holy Father's comment at the General Audience of 14 October 1981 on "What Happened in May: A Great Divine Trial" should be recalled: *Insegnamenti di Giovanni Paolo II*, IV, 2 (Vatican City, 1981), 409-412.

human family, which with affectionate love we entrust to you, O Mother. May there dawn for everyone the time of peace and freedom, the time of truth, of justice and of hope."[3]

In order to respond more fully to the requests of "Our Lady," the Holy Father desired to make more explicit during the Holy Year of the Redemption the Act of Entrustment of 7 May 1981, which had been repeated in Fatima on 13 May 1982. On 25 March 1984 in Saint Peter's Square, while recalling the fiat uttered by Mary at the Annunciation, the Holy Father, in spiritual union with the Bishops of the world, who had been "convoked" beforehand, entrusted all men and women and all peoples to the Immaculate Heart of Mary, in terms which recalled the heartfelt words spoken in 1981:

"*O Mother of all men and women, and of all peoples*, you who know all their sufferings and their hopes, you who have a mother's awareness of all the struggles between good and evil, between light and darkness, which afflict the modern world, accept the cry which we, moved by the Holy Spirit, address directly to your Heart. *Embrace* with the *love* of the Mother and Handmaid of the Lord, this human world of ours, which we entrust and consecrate to you, for we are full of concern for the earthly and eternal destiny of individuals and peoples.

"In a special way we entrust and consecrate to you those individuals and nations which particularly need to be thus entrusted and consecrated.

"We have recourse to your protection, holy Mother of God! *Despise not our petitions in our necessities.*"

The Pope then continued more forcefully and with more specific references, as though commenting on the Message of Fatima in its sorrowful fulfillment:

For All Time

"Behold, as we stand before you, Mother of Christ, before your Immaculate Heart, we desire, together with the whole Church, to unite ourselves with the consecra-

---

[3] Radio message during the Ceremony of Veneration, Thanksgiving, and Entrustment to the Virgin Mary Theotokos in the Basilica of Saint Mary Major: Insegnamenti di Giovanni Paolo II, IV, 1 (Vatican City, 1981), 1246.

tion which, for love of us, your Son made of himself to the Father: 'For their sake', He said, 'I consecrate Myself that they also may be consecrated in the truth' (Jn 17:19). We wish to unite ourselves with our Redeemer in this His consecration for the world and for the human race, which, in His divine Heart, has the power to obtain pardon and to secure reparation.

"*The power of this consecration* lasts for all time and embraces all individuals, peoples and nations. It overcomes every evil that the spirit of darkness is able to awaken, and has in fact awakened in our times, in the heart of man and in his history.

"How deeply we feel the need for the consecration of humanity and the world—our modern world—in union with Christ Himself! For the redeeming work of Christ must be *shared in by the world through the Church.*

"The present Year of the Redemption shows this: the special Jubilee of the whole Church.

"*Above all creatures*, may you be blessed, you, the Handmaid of the Lord, who in the fullest way obeyed the divine call!

"Hail to you, who *are wholly united* to the redeeming consecration of your Son!

"Mother of the Church! Enlighten the People of God along the paths of faith, hope, and love! Enlighten especially the peoples whose consecration and entrustment by us you are awaiting. Help us to live in the truth of the consecration of Christ for the entire human family of the modern world.

"In entrusting to you, O Mother, the world, all individuals and peoples, we also *entrust* to you *this very consecration of the world*, placing it in your motherly Heart.

From Nuclear War, Deliver Us!

"Immaculate Heart! Help us to conquer the menace of evil, which so easily takes root in the hearts of the people of today, and whose immeasurable effects already weigh down upon our modern world and seem to block the paths towards the future!

"From famine and war, *deliver us.*

"From nuclear war, from incalculable self-destruction, from every kind of war, *deliver us.*

"From sins against the life of man from its very beginning, *deliver us.*

"From hatred and from the demeaning of the dignity of the children of God, *deliver us.*

"From every kind of injustice in the life of society, both national and international, *deliver us.*

"From readiness to trample on the commandments of God, *deliver us.*

"From attempts to stifle in human hearts the very truth of God, *deliver us.*

"From the loss of awareness of good and evil, *deliver us.*

"From sins against the Holy Spirit, *deliver us, deliver us.*

"Accept, O Mother of Christ, this cry *laden with the sufferings* of all individual human beings, *laden with the sufferings* of whole societies.

"Help us with the power of the Holy Spirit to conquer all sin: individual sin and the 'sin of the world', sin in all its manifestations.

"Let there be revealed, once more, in the history of the world the infinite saving power of the Redemption: the power of *merciful Love!* May it put a stop to evil! May it transform consciences! May your Immaculate Heart reveal for all the *light of Hope!*"[4]

Sister Lucia personally confirmed that this solemn and universal act of consecration corresponded to what Our Lady wished (*"Sim, està feita, tal como Nossa Senhora a pediu, desde o dia 25 de Março de 1984"*: "Yes it has been done just as Our Lady asked, on 25 March 1984," Letter of 8 November 1989). Hence any further discussion or request is without basis.

---

[4] On the Jubilee Day for Families, the Pope entrusted individuals and nations to Our Lady: Insegnamenti di Giovanni Paolo II, VII, 1 (Vatican City, 1984), 775-777.

The "Secret" of Fatima

First and Second Parts of the "Secret"[5]
from Sister Lucia's "Third Memoir"
Addressed to the Bishop of Leiria-Fatima
(August 31, 1941)

THIS WILL ENTAIL MY speaking about the Secret, and thus answering the first question. What is the secret? It seems to me that I can reveal it, since I already have permission from Heaven to do so. God's representatives on earth have authorized me to do this several times and in various letters, one of which, I believe, is in your keeping. This letter is from Father José Bernardo Gonçalves, and in it he advises me to write to the Holy Father, suggesting, among other things, that I should reveal the Secret. I did say something about it. But in order not to make my letter too long, since I was told to keep it short, I confined myself to the essentials, leaving it to God to provide another more favorable opportunity.

In my second account, I have already described in detail the doubt which tormented me from 13 June until 13 July, and how it disappeared completely during the Apparition on that day.

Well, the Secret is made up of three distinct parts, two of which I am now going to reveal.

The first part is the vision of Hell.

Our Lady showed us a great sea of fire which seemed to be under the earth. Plunged in this fire were demons and souls in human form, like transparent burning embers, all blackened or burnished bronze, floating about in

---

[5] In the "Fourth Memoir" of 8 December 1941, Sister Lucia writes: "I shall begin then my new task, and thus fulfil the commands received from Your Excellency as well as the desires of Dr. Galamba. With the exception of that part of the Secret which I am not permitted to reveal at present, I shall say everything. I shall not knowingly omit anything, though I suppose I may forget just a few small details of minor importance."

the conflagration, now raised into the air by the flames that issued from within themselves together with great clouds of smoke, now falling back on every side like sparks in a huge fire, without weight or equilibrium, and amid shrieks and groans of pain and despair, which horrified us and made us tremble with fear. The demons could be distinguished by their terrifying and repulsive likeness to frightful and unknown animals, all black and transparent. This vision lasted but an instant. How can we ever be grateful enough to our kind heavenly Mother, who had already prepared us by promising, in the first Apparition, to take us to heaven. Otherwise, I think we would have died of fear and terror.

We then looked up at Our Lady, who said to us so kindly and so sadly:

Various Nations will be Annihilated

"You have seen Hell where the souls of poor sinners go. To save them, God wishes to establish in the world devotion to my Immaculate Heart. If what I say to you is done, many souls will be saved and there will be peace. The war is going to end: but if people do not cease offending God, a worse one will break out during the Pontificate of Pius XI. When you see a night illumined by an unknown light, know that this is the great sign given you by God that He is about to punish the world for its crimes, by means of war, famine, and persecutions of the Church and of the Holy Father. To prevent this, I shall come to ask for the consecration of Russia to my Immaculate Heart, and the Communion of reparation on the First Saturdays. If my requests are heeded, Russia will be converted, and there will be peace; if not, she will spread her errors throughout the world, causing wars and persecutions of the Church. The good will be martyred; the Holy Father will have much to suffer; various nations will be annihilated. In the end, my Immaculate Heart will triumph. The Holy Father will consecrate Russia to me, and she shall be converted, and a period of peace will be granted to the world."[6]

---

[6] In the "Fourth Memoir" Sister Lucia adds: "In Portugal, the dogma of the faith will always be preserved, etc. ...."

Third Part of the "Secret"[7]
Revealed at the Cova da Iria-Fatima,
on 13 July 1917.

I WRITE IN OBEDIENCE TO YOU, my God, Who command me to do so through his Excellency the Bishop of Leiria and through Your Most Holy Mother and mine.

After the two parts which I have already explained, at the left of Our Lady and a little above, we saw an Angel with a flaming sword in his left hand; flashing, it gave out flames that looked as though they would set the world on fire; but they died out in contact with the splendor that Our Lady radiated towards him from her right hand: pointing to the earth with his right hand, the Angel cried out in a loud voice: 'Penance, Penance, Penance!'. And we saw in an immense light that is God: 'something similar to how people appear in a mirror when they pass in front of it' a Bishop dressed in White 'we had the impression that it was the Holy Father'. Other Bishops, Priests, men and women Religious going up a steep mountain, at the top of which there was a big Cross of rough-hewn trunks as of a cork-tree with the bark; before reaching there the Holy Father passed through a big city half in ruins and half trembling with halting step, afflicted with pain and sorrow, he prayed for the souls of the corpses he met on his way; having reached the top of the mountain, on his knees at the foot of the big Cross he was killed by a group of soldiers who fired bullets and arrows at him, and in the same way there died one after another the other Bishops, Priests, men and women Religious, and various lay people of different ranks and positions. Beneath the two arms of the Cross there were two Angels each with a crystal aspersorium in his hand, in which they gathered up the blood of the Martyrs and with it sprinkled the souls that were making their way to God.

Tuy-3-1-1944."

---

[7] In the translation, the original text has been respected, even as regards the imprecise punctuation, which nevertheless does not impede an understanding of what the visionary wished to say.

Letter of His Holiness Pope John Paul II to Sister Lucia

To the Reverend Sister Maria Lucia of the Convent of Coimbra

IN THE GREAT JOY OF EASTER, I greet you with the words the Risen Jesus spoke to the disciples: "Peace be with you!" I will be happy to be able to meet you on the long-awaited day of the Beatification of Francisco and Jacinta, which, please God, I will celebrate on 13 May of this year.

Since on that day there will be time only for a brief greeting and not a conversation, I am sending His Excellency Archbishop Tarcisio Bertone, Secretary of the Congregation for the Doctrine of the Faith, to speak with you. This is the Congregation which works most closely with the Pope in defending the true Catholic faith, and which since 1957, as you know, has kept your handwritten letter containing the third part of the "Secret" revealed on 13 July 1917 at Cova da Iria, Fatima.

Archbishop Bertone, accompanied by the Bishop of Leiria, His Excellency Bishop Serafim de Sousa Ferreira e Silva, will come in my name to ask certain questions about the interpretation of "the third part of the Secret."

Sister Maria Lucia, you may speak openly and candidly to Archbishop Bertone, who will report your answers directly to me.

I pray fervently to the Mother of the Risen Lord for you, Reverend Sister, for the Community of Coimbra and for the whole Church. May Mary, Mother of pilgrim humanity, keep us always united to Jesus, her beloved Son and our brother, the Lord of life and glory.

With my special Apostolic Blessing.

POPE JOHN PAUL II
From the Vatican, 19 April 2000

Conversation of Archbishop Bertone with Sister Lucia

THE MEETING between Sister Lucia, Archbishop Tarcisio Bertone, Secretary of the Congregation for the Doctrine of the Faith, sent by the Holy Father, and Bishop Serafim de Sousa Ferreira e Silva, Bishop of Leiria-Fatima, took place on Thursday, 27 April 2000, in the Carmel of Saint Teresa in Coimbra.

Sister Lucia was lucid and at ease; she was very happy that the Holy Father was going to Fatima for the Beatification of Francisco and Jacinta, something she had looked forward to for a long time.

The Bishop of Leiria-Fatima read the autograph letter of the Holy Father, which explained the reasons for the visit. Sister Lucia felt honoured by this and reread the letter herself, contemplating it in own her hands. She said that she was prepared to answer all questions frankly.

Verifies the Secret

At this point, Archbishop Bertone presented two envelopes to her: the first containing the second, which held the third part of the "Secret" of Fatima. Immediately, touching it with her fingers, she said: "This is my letter," and then while reading it: "This is my writing."

The original text, in Portuguese, was read and interpreted with the help of the Bishop of Leiria-Fatima. Sister Lucia agreed with the interpretation that the third part of the "Secret" was a prophetic vision, similar to those in sacred history. She repeated her conviction that the vision of Fatima concerns above all the struggle of atheistic Communism against the Church and against Christians, and describes the terrible sufferings of the victims of the faith in the twentieth century.

When asked: "Is the principal figure in the vision the Pope?," Sister Lucia replied at once that it was. She recalled that the three children were very sad about the suffering of the Pope, and that Jacinta kept saying: "Coitadinho do Santo Padre, tenho muita pena dos pecadores!" ("Poor Holy Father, I am very sad for sinners!"). Sister Lucia continued: "We did not know the name of the

Pope; Our Lady did not tell us the name of the Pope; we did not know whether it was Benedict XV or Pius XII or Paul VI or John Paul II; but it was the Pope who was suffering and that made us suffer too."

As regards the passage about the Bishop dressed in white, that is, the Holy Father—as the children immediately realized during the "vision"—who is struck dead and falls to the ground, Sister Lucia was in full agreement with the Pope's claim that "it was a mother's hand that guided the bullet's path and in his throes the Pope halted at the threshold of death" (Pope John Paul II, Meditation from the Policlinico Gemelli to the Italian Bishops, 13 May 1994).

Only Later Would Be Understood

Before giving the sealed envelope containing the third part of the "Secret" to the then Bishop of Leiria-Fatima, Sister Lucia wrote on the outside envelope that it could be opened only after 1960, either by the Patriarch of Lisbon or the Bishop of Leiria. Archbishop Bertone therefore asked: "Why only after 1960? Was it Our Lady who fixed that date?" Sister Lucia replied: "It was not Our Lady. I fixed the date because I had the intuition that before 1960 it would not be understood, but that only later would it be understood. Now it can be better understood. I wrote down what I saw; however it was not for me to interpret it, but for the Pope.

Finally, mention was made of the unpublished manuscript which Sister Lucia has prepared as a reply to the many letters that come from Marian devotees and from pilgrims. The work is called *Os apelos da Mensagem de Fatima*, and it gathers together in the style of catechesis and exhortation thoughts and reflections which express Sister Lucia's feelings and her clear and unaffected spirituality. She was asked if she would be happy to have it published, and she replied: "If the Holy Father agrees, then I am happy, otherwise I obey whatever the Holy Father decides." Sister Lucia wants to present the text for ecclesiastical approval, and she hopes that what she has written will help to guide men and women of good will along the path that leads to God, the final goal of every human longing. The conversation ends with an exchange of rosaries. Sister Lucia is given a rosary sent by the Holy Father, and she in turn offers a number of rosaries made by herself.

The meeting concludes with the blessing imparted in the name of the Holy Father.

Announcement Made by Cardinal Angelo Sodano, Secretary of State

At the end of the Mass presided over by the Holy Father at Fatima, May 13, 2000

BROTHERS AND SISTERS in the Lord! At the conclusion of this solemn celebration, I feel bound to offer our beloved Holy Father Pope John Paul II, on behalf of all present, heartfelt good wishes for his approaching 80th Birthday and to thank him for his vital pastoral ministry for the good of all God's Holy Church; we present the heartfelt wishes of the whole Church.

On this solemn occasion of his visit to Fatima, His Holiness has directed me to make an announcement to you. As you know, the purpose of his visit to Fatima has been to beatify the two "little shepherds." Nevertheless he also wishes his pilgrimage to be a renewed gesture of gratitude to Our Lady for her protection during these years of his papacy. This protection seems also to be linked to the so-called third part of the "Secret" of Fatima.

That text contains a prophetic vision similar to those found in Sacred Scripture, which do not describe photographically the details of future events, but synthesize and compress against a single background facts which extend through time in an unspecified succession and duration. As a result, the text must be interpreted in a symbolic key.

The vision of Fatima concerns above all the war waged by atheistic systems against the Church and Christians, and it describes the immense suffering endured by the witnesses of the faith in the last century of the second millennium. It is an interminable Way of the Cross led by the Popes of the twentieth century.

According to the interpretation of the "little shepherds," which was also confirmed recently by Sister Lucia, "the Bishop clothed in white" who prays for all the faithful is the Pope. As he makes his way with great difficulty towards the Cross amid the corpses of those who were martyred (Bishops, priests, men and women Religious and many lay people), he too falls to the ground, apparently dead, under a hail of gunfire.

After the assassination attempt of 13 May 1981, it appeared evident that it was "a mother's hand that guided the bullet's path," enabling "the Pope in his throes" to halt "at the threshold of death" (Pope John Paul II, Meditation from the Policlinico Gemelli to the Italian Bishops, Insegnamenti, XVII, 1 [1994], 1061). On the occasion of a visit to Rome by the then Bishop of Leiria-Fatima, the Pope decided to give him the bullet which had remained in the jeep after the assassination attempt, so that it might be kept in the shrine. By the Bishop's decision, the bullet was later set in the crown of the statue of Our Lady of Fatima.

They Tragically Continue

The successive events of 1989 led, both in the Soviet Union and in a number of countries of Eastern Europe, to the fall of the Communist regimes which promoted atheism. For this too His Holiness offers heartfelt thanks to the Most Holy Virgin. In other parts of the world, however, attacks against the Church and against Christians, with the burden of suffering they bring, tragically continue. Even if the events to which the third part of the "Secret" of Fatima refers now seem part of the past, Our Lady's call to conversion and penance, issued at the start of the twentieth century, remains timely and urgent today. "The Lady of the message seems to read the signs of the times—the signs of our time—with special insight... The insistent invitation of Mary Most Holy to penance is nothing but the manifestation of her maternal concern for the fate of the human family, in need of conversion and forgiveness" (Pope John Paul II, Message for the 1997 World Day of the Sick, No. 1, Insegnamenti, XIX, 2 [1996], 561).

In order that the faithful may better receive the message of Our Lady of Fatima, the Pope has charged the Congregation for the Doctrine of the Faith with making public the third part of the "Secret," after the preparation of an appropriate commentary.

Brothers and sisters, let us thank Our Lady of Fatima for her protection. To her maternal intercession let us entrust the Church of the Third Millennium.

Sub tuum praesidium confugimus, Sancta Dei Genetrix! Intercede pro Ecclesia. Intercede pro Papa nostro Ioanne Paulo II. Amen.

Fatima, 13 May 2000

Theological Commentary

A CAREFUL READING OF THE TEXT of the so-called third "Secret" of Fatima, published here in its entirety long after the fact and by decision of the Holy Father, will probably prove disappointing or surprising after all the speculation it has stirred. No great mystery is revealed; nor is the future unveiled. We see the Church of the martyrs of the century which has just passed represented in a scene described in a language which is symbolic and not easy to decipher. Is this what the Mother of the Lord wished to communicate to Christianity and to humanity at a time of great difficulty and distress? Is it of any help to us at the beginning of the new millennium? Or are these only projections of the inner world of children, brought up in a climate of profound piety but shaken at the same time by the tempests which threatened their own time? How should we understand the vision? What are we to make of it?

Public Revelation and private revelations – their theological status.

Before attempting an interpretation, the main lines of which can be found in the statement read by Cardinal Sodano on 13 May of this year at the end of the Mass celebrated by the Holy Father in Fatima, there is a need for some basic clarification of the way in which, according to Church teaching, phenomena such as Fatima are to be understood within the life of faith. The teaching of the Church distinguishes between "public Revelation" and "private revelations." The two realities differ not only in degree but also in essence. The term "public Revelation" refers to the revealing action of God directed to humanity as a whole and which finds its literary expression in the two parts of the Bible: the Old and New Testaments. It is called "Revelation" because in it God gradually made himself known to men, to the point of becoming man himself, in order to draw to himself the whole world and unite it with himself through his Incarnate Son, Jesus Christ. It is not a matter therefore of intellectual communication, but of a life-giving process in which God comes to meet man. At the same time this process naturally produces data pertaining to the mind and to the understanding of the mystery of God. It is a process which involves man in his entirety and therefore reason as well, but not reason alone. Because God is one, history, which he shares with humanity, is also one. It is valid for all time, and it has reached its fulfillment in the life, death and resurrection of Jesus Christ. In Christ, God has said everything, that is, he has revealed himself completely, and therefore Revelation came to an end with the fulfillment of the mystery of Christ as enunciated in the New Testament. To explain the finality and completeness of Revelation, the Catechism of the Catholic Church quotes a text of Saint John of the Cross: "In giving us his Son, his only Word (for he possesses no other), he spoke everything to us at once in this sole Word—and he has no more to say... because what he spoke before to the prophets in parts, he has now spoken all at once by giving us the All Who is His Son. Any person questioning God or desiring some vision or revelation would be guilty not only of foolish behavior but also of offending him, by not fixing his eyes entirely upon Christ and by living with the desire for some other novelty" (No. 65; Saint John of the Cross, *The Ascent of Mount Carmel*, II, 22).

Because the single Revelation of God addressed to all peoples comes to completion with Christ and the witness borne to him in the books of the New Testament, the Church is tied to this unique event of sacred history and to the word of the Bible, which guarantees and interprets it. But this does not mean that the Church can now look only to the past and that she is condemned to sterile repetition. The Catechism of the Catholic Church says in this regard: "...even if Revelation is already complete, it has not been made fully explicit; it remains for Christian faith gradually to grasp its full significance over the course of the centuries" (No. 66).

The way in which the Church is bound to both the uniqueness of the event and progress in understanding it is very well illustrated in the farewell discourse of the Lord when, taking leave of his disciples, he says: "I have yet many things to say to you, but you cannot bear them now. When the Spirit of truth comes, he will guide you into all the truth; for he will not speak on his own authority... He will glorify me, for he will take what is mine and declare it to you" (Jn 16:12-14). On the one hand, the Spirit acts as a guide who discloses a knowledge previously unreachable because the premise was missing—this is the boundless breadth and depth of Christian faith. On the other hand, to be guided by the Spirit is also "to draw from" the riches of Jesus Christ himself, the inexhaustible depths of which appear in the way the Spirit leads. In this regard, the Catechism cites profound words of Pope Gregory the Great: "The sacred Scriptures grow with the one who reads them" (No. 94; Gregory the Great, *Homilia in Ezechielem* I, 7, 8). The Second Vatican Council notes three essential ways in which the Spirit guides in the Church, and therefore three ways in which "the word grows": through the meditation and study of the faithful, through the deep understanding which comes from spiritual experience, and through the preaching of "those who, in the succession of the episcopate, have received the sure charism of truth" (Dei Verbum, 8).

In this context, it now becomes possible to understand rightly the concept of "private revelation," which refers to all the visions and revelations which have taken place since the completion of the New Testament. This is the category to which we must assign the message of Fatima. In this respect, let us listen once again to the Catechism of the Catholic Church: "Throughout the ages, there have been so-called 'private' revelations, some of which have been recognized by the authority of the Church... It is not their role to complete Christ's definitive Revelation, but to help live more fully by it in a certain period of history" (No. 67). This clarifies two things:

1. The authority of private revelations is essentially different from that of the definitive public Revelation. The latter demands faith; in it in fact God himself speaks to us through human words and the mediation of the living community of the Church. Faith in God and in his word is different from any other human faith, trust or opinion. The certainty that it is God who is speaking gives me the assurance that I am in touch with truth itself. It gives me a certitude which is beyond verification by any human way of knowing. It is the certitude upon which I build my life and to which I entrust myself in dying.

2. Private revelation is a help to this faith, and shows its credibility precisely by leading me back to the definitive public Revelation. In this regard, Cardinal Prospero Lambertini, the future Pope Benedict XIV, says in his classic treatise, which later became normative for beatifications and canonizations: "An assent of Catholic faith is not due to revelations approved in this way; it is not even possible. These revelations seek rather an assent of human faith in keeping with the requirements of prudence, which puts them before us as probable and credible to piety." The Flemish theologian E. Dhanis, an eminent scholar in this field, states succinctly that ecclesiastical approval of a private revelation has three elements: the message contains nothing contrary to faith or morals; it is lawful to make it public; and the faithful are authorized to accept it with prudence (E. Dhanis, Sguardo su Fatima e bilancio di una discussione, in La Civiltà Cattolica 104 [1953], II, 392-406, in particular 397). Such a message can be a genuine help in understanding the Gospel and living it better at a particular moment in time; therefore, it should not be disregarded. It is a help which is offered, but which one is not obliged to use.

The criterion for the truth and value of a private revelation is therefore its orientation to Christ himself. When it leads us away from him, when it becomes independent of him or even presents itself as another and better plan of salvation, more important than the Gospel, then it certainly does not come from the Holy Spirit, who guides us more deeply into the Gospel and not away from it. This does not mean that a private revelation will not offer new emphases or give rise to new devotional forms, or deepen and spread older forms. But in all of this there must be a nurturing of faith, hope and love, which are the unchanging path to salvation for everyone.

We might add that private revelations often spring from popular piety and leave their stamp on it, giving it a new impulse and opening the way for new forms of it. Nor does this exclude that they will have an effect even on the liturgy, as we see for instance in the feasts of Corpus Christi and of the Sacred Heart of Jesus. From one point of view, the relationship between Revelation and private revelations appears in the relationship between the liturgy and popular piety: the liturgy is the criterion, it is the living form of the Church as a whole, fed directly by the Gospel. Popular piety is a sign that the faith is spreading its roots into the heart of a people in such a way that it reaches into daily life. Popular religiosity is the first and fundamental mode of "inculturation" of the faith. While it must always take its lead and direction from the liturgy, it in turn enriches the faith by involving the heart.

We have thus moved from the somewhat negative clarifications, initially needed, to a positive definition of private revelations. How can they be classified correctly in relation to Scripture? To which theological category do they belong? The oldest letter of Saint Paul which has been preserved, perhaps the oldest of the New Testament texts, the First Letter to the Thessalonians, seems to me to point the way. The Apostle says: "Do not quench the Spirit, do not despise prophesying, but test everything, holding fast to what is good" (5:19-21). In every age the Church has received the charism of prophecy, which must be scrutinized but not scorned. On this point, it should be kept in mind that prophecy in the biblical sense does not mean to predict the future but to explain the will of God for the present, and therefore show the right path to take for the future. A person who foretells what is going to happen responds to the curiosity of the mind, which wants to draw back the veil on the future. The prophet speaks to the blindness of will and of reason, and declares the will of God as an indication and demand for the present time. In this case, prediction of the future is of secondary importance. What is essential is the actualization of the definitive Revelation, which concerns me at the deepest level. The prophetic word is a warning or a consolation, or both together. In this sense there is a link between the charism of prophecy and the category of "the signs of the times," which Vatican II brought to light anew: "You know how to interpret the appearance of earth and sky; why then do you not know how to interpret the present time?" (Lk 12:56). In this saying of Jesus, the "signs of the times" must be understood as the path he was taking, indeed it must be understood as Jesus himself. To interpret the signs of the times in the light of faith means to recognize the presence of Christ in every age. In the private revelations approved by the Church—and therefore also in Fatima—this is the point: they help us to understand the signs of the times and to respond to them rightly in faith.

The Anthropological Structure of Private Revelations

In these reflections we have sought so far to identify the theological status of private revelations. Before undertaking an interpretation of the message of Fatima, we must still attempt briefly to offer some clarification of their anthropological (psychological) character. In this field, theological anthropology distinguishes three forms of perception or "vision": vision with the senses, and hence exterior bodily perception, interior perception, and spiritual vision (visio sensibilis - imaginativa - intellectualis). It is clear that in the visions of Lourdes, Fatima and other places it is not a question of normal exterior perception of the senses: the images and forms which are seen are not located spatially, as is the case for example with a tree or a house. This is perfectly obvious, for instance, as regards the vision of Hell (described in the first part of the Fatima "Secret") or even the vision described in the third part of the "Secret."

But the same can be very easily shown with regard to other visions, especially since not everybody present saw them, but only the "visionaries." It is also clear that it is not a matter of a "vision" in the mind, without images, as occurs at the higher levels of mysticism. Therefore we are dealing with the middle category, interior perception. For the visionary, this perception certainly has the force of a presence, equivalent for that person to an external manifestation to the senses.

Interior vision does not mean fantasy, which would be no more than an expression of the subjective imagination. It means rather that the soul is touched by something real, even if beyond the senses. It is rendered capable of seeing that which is beyond the senses, that which cannot be seen—seeing by means of the "interior senses." It involves true "objects," which touch the soul, even if these "objects" do not belong to our habitual sensory world.

This is why there is a need for an interior vigilance of the heart, which is usually precluded by the intense pressure of external reality and of the images and thoughts which fill the soul. The person is led beyond pure exteriority and is touched by deeper dimensions of reality, which become visible to him. Perhaps this explains why children tend to be the ones to receive these apparitions: their souls are as yet little disturbed, their interior powers of perception are still not impaired. "On the lips of children and of babes you have found praise," replies Jesus with a phrase of Psalm 8 (v. 3) to the criticism of the High Priests and elders, who had judged the children's cries of "hosanna" inappropriate (cf. Mt 21:16).

"Interior vision" is not fantasy but, as we have said, a true and valid means of verification. But it also has its limitations. Even in exterior vision the subjective element is always present. We do not see the pure object, but it comes to us through the filter of our senses, which carry out a work of translation. This is still more evident in the case of interior vision, especially when it involves realities which in themselves transcend our horizon. The subject, the visionary, is still more powerfully involved. He sees insofar as he is able, in the modes of representation and consciousness available to him. In the case of interior vision, the process of translation is even more extensive than in exterior vision, for the subject shares in an essential way in the formation of the image of what appears. He can arrive at the image only within the bounds of his capacities and possibilities.

Such visions therefore are never simple "photographs" of the other world, but are influenced by the potentialities and limitations of the perceiving subject.

This can be demonstrated in all the great visions of the saints; and naturally it is also true of the visions of the children at Fatima. The images described by them are by no means a simple expression of their fantasy, but the result of a real perception of a higher and interior origin.

But neither should they be thought of as if for a moment the veil of the other world were drawn back, with heaven appearing in its pure essence, as one day we hope to see it in our definitive union with God. Rather the images are, in a manner of speaking, a synthesis of the impulse coming from on high and the capacity to receive this impulse in the visionaries, that is, the children. For this reason, the figurative language of the visions is symbolic.

In this regard, Cardinal Sodano stated: "[they] do not describe photographically the details of future events, but synthesize and compress against a single background facts which extend through time in an unspecified succession and duration."

This compression of time and place in a single image

is typical of such visions, which for the most part can be deciphered only in retrospect. Not every element of the vision has to have a specific historical sense. It is the vision as a whole that matters, and the details must be understood on the basis of the images taken in their entirety. The central element of the image is revealed where it coincides with what is the focal point of Christian "prophecy" itself: the center is found where the vision becomes a summons and a guide to the will of God.

An Attempt to Interpret the "Secret" of Fatima

The first and second parts of the "Secret" of Fatima have already been so amply discussed in the relative literature that there is no need to deal with them again here. I would just like to recall briefly the most significant point. For one terrible moment, the children were given a vision of Hell. They saw the fall of "the souls of poor sinners." And now they are told why they have been exposed to this moment: "in order to save souls"—to show the way to salvation. The words of the First Letter of Peter come to mind: "As the outcome of your faith you obtain the salvation of your souls" (1:9). To reach this goal, the way indicated — surprisingly for people from the Anglo-Saxon and German cultural world—is devotion to the Immaculate Heart of Mary. A brief comment may suffice to explain this. In biblical language, the "heart" indicates the center of human life, the point where reason, will, temperament and sensitivity converge, where the person finds his unity and his interior orientation. According to Matthew 5:8, the "immaculate heart" is a heart which, with God's Grace, has come to perfect interior unity and therefore "sees God." To be "devoted" to the Immaculate Heart of Mary means therefore to embrace this attitude of heart, which makes the fiat— "your will be done"—the defining center of one's whole life. It might be objected that we should not place a human being between ourselves and Christ. But then we remember that Paul did not hesitate to say to his communities: "imitate me" (1 Cor 4:16; Phil 3:17; 1 Th 1:6; 2 Th 3:7, 9). In the Apostle they could see concretely what it meant to follow Christ. But from whom might we better learn in every age than from the Mother of the Lord?

Thus we come finally to the third part of the "Secret" of Fatima which for the first time is being published in its entirety. As is clear from the documentation presented here, the interpretation offered by Cardinal Sodano in his statement of 13 May was first put personally to Sister Lucia.

Sister Lucia responded by pointing out that she had received the vision but not its interpretation. The interpretation, she said, belonged not to the visionary but to the Church. After reading the text, however, she said that this interpretation corresponded to what she had experienced and that on her part she thought the interpretation correct. In what follows, therefore, we can only attempt to provide a deeper foundation for this interpretation, on the basis of the criteria already considered.

"To save souls" has emerged as the key word of the first and second parts of the "Secret," and the key word of this third part is the threefold cry: "Penance, Penance, Penance!" The beginning of the Gospel comes to mind: "Repent and believe the Good News" (Mk 1:15). To understand the signs of the times means to accept the urgency of penance — of conversion — of faith. This is the correct response to this moment of history, characterized by the grave perils outlined in the images that follow. Allow me to add here a personal recollection: in a conversation with me, Sister Lucia said that it appeared ever more clearly to her that the purpose of all the apparitions was to help people to grow more and more in faith, hope, and love— everything else was intended to lead to this.

Let us now examine more closely the single images. The Angel with the flaming sword on the left of the Mother of God recalls similar images in the Book of Revelation. This represents the threat of judgment which looms over the world. Today the prospect that the world might be reduced to ashes by a sea of fire no longer seems pure fantasy: man himself, with his inventions, has forged the flaming sword. The vision then shows the power which stands opposed to the force of destruction—the splendor of the Mother of God and, stemming from this in a certain way, the summons to penance. In this way, the importance of human freedom is underlined: the future is not in fact unchangeably set, and the image which the children saw is in no way a film preview of a future in which nothing can be changed. Indeed, the whole point of the vision is to bring freedom onto the scene and to steer freedom in a positive direction. The purpose of the vision is not to show a film of an irrevocably fixed future. Its meaning is exactly the opposite: it is meant to mobilize the forces of change in the right direction. Therefore we must totally discount fatalistic explanations of the "Secret," such as, for example, the claim that the would-be assassin of 13 May 1981 was merely an instrument of the divine plan guided by Providence and could not therefore have acted freely, or other similar ideas in circulation. Rather, the vision speaks of dangers and how we might be saved from them.

The next phrases of the text show very clearly once again the symbolic character of the vision: God remains immeasurable, and is the light which surpasses every vision of ours. Human persons appear as in a mirror. We must always keep in mind the limits in the vision itself, which here are indicated visually. The future appears only "in a mirror dimly" (1 Cor 13:12). Let us now consider the individual images which follow in the text of the "Secret." The place of the action is described in three symbols: a steep mountain, a great city reduced to ruins and finally a large rough-hewn cross. The mountain and city symbolize the arena of human history: history as an arduous ascent to the summit, history as the arena of human creativity and social harmony, but at the same time a place of destruction, where man actually destroys the fruits of his own work. The city can be the place of communion and progress, but also of danger and the most extreme menace. On the mountain stands the cross—the goal and guide of history. The cross transforms destruction into salvation; it stands as a sign of history's misery but also as a promise for history.

At this point human persons appear: the Bishop dressed in white ("we had the impression that it was the Holy Father"), other Bishops, priests, men and women Religious, and men and women of different ranks and social positions. The Pope seems to precede the others, trembling and suffering because of all the horrors around him. Not only do the houses of the city lie half in ruins, but he makes his way among the corpses of the dead. The Church's path is thus described as a Via Crucis, as a journey through a time of violence, destruction and persecution. The history of an entire century can be seen represented in this image. Just as the places of the earth are synthetically described in the two images of the mountain and the city, and are directed towards the cross, so too time is presented in a compressed way. In the vision we can recognize the last century as a century of martyrs, a century of suffering and persecution for the Church, a century of World Wars and the many local wars which filled the last fifty years and have inflicted unprecedented forms of cruelty. In the "mirror" of this vision we see passing before us the witnesses of the faith decade by decade. Here it would be appropriate to mention a phrase from the letter which Sister Lucia wrote to the Holy Father on 12 May 1982: "The third part of the 'Secret' refers to Our Lady's words: 'If not, [Russia] will spread her errors throughout the world, causing wars and persecutions of the Church. The good will be martyred; the Holy Father will have much to suffer; various nations will be annihilated'."

In the Via Crucis of an entire century, the figure of the Pope has a special role. In his arduous ascent of the mountain we can undoubtedly see a convergence of different Popes. Beginning from Pius X up to the present Pope, they all shared the sufferings of the century and strove to go forward through all the anguish along the path which leads to the Cross. In the vision, the Pope too is killed along with the martyrs. When, after the attempted assassination on 13 May 1981, the Holy Father had the text of the third part of the "Secret" brought to him, was it not inevitable that he should see in it his own fate? He had been very close to death, and he himself explained his survival in the following words: "... it was a mother's hand that guided the bullet's path and in his throes the Pope halted at the threshold of death" (13 May 1994). That here "a mother's hand" had deflected the fateful bullet only shows once more that there is no immutable destiny, that faith and prayer are forces which can influence history and that in the end prayer is more powerful than bullets and faith more powerful than armies.

The concluding part of the "Secret" uses images which Lucia may have seen in devotional books and which draw their inspiration from long-standing intuitions of faith. It is a consoling vision, which seeks to open a history of blood and tears to the healing power of God. Beneath the arms of the cross angels gather up the blood of the martyrs, and with it they give life to the souls making their way to God. Here, the blood of Christ and the blood of the martyrs are considered as one: the blood of the martyrs runs down from the arms of the cross. The martyrs die in communion with the Passion of Christ, and their death becomes one with his. For the sake of the body of Christ, they complete what is still lacking in his afflictions (cf. Col 1:24). Their life has itself become a Eucharist, part of the mystery of the grain of wheat which in dying yields abundant fruit. The blood of the martyrs is the seed of Christians, said Tertullian. As from Christ's death, from his wounded side, the Church was born, so the death of the witnesses is fruitful for the future life of the Church. Therefore, the vision of the third part of the "Secret," so distressing at first, concludes with an image of hope: no suffering is in vain, and it is a suffering Church, a Church of martyrs, which becomes a signpost for man in his search for God. The loving arms of God welcome not only those who suffer like Lazarus, who found great solace there and mysteriously represents Christ, who wished to become for us the poor Lazarus. There is something more: from the suffering of the witnesses there comes a purifying and renewing power, because their suffering is the actualization of the suffering of Christ himself and a communication in the here and now of its saving effect.

And so we come to the final question: What is the meaning of the "Secret" of Fatima as a whole (in its three parts)? What does it say to us? First of all we must affirm with Cardinal Sodano: "... the events to which the third part of the 'Secret' of Fatima refers now seem part of the past." Insofar as individual events are described, they belong to the past. Those who expected exciting apocalyptic revelations about the end of the world or the future course of history are bound to be disappointed. Fatima does not satisfy our curiosity in this way, just as Christian faith in general cannot be reduced to an object of mere curiosity. What remains was already evident when we began our reflections on the text of the "Secret": the exhortation to prayer as the path of "salvation for souls" and, likewise, the summons to penance and conversion.

Stronger Than Guns and Weapons

I would like finally to mention another key expression of the "Secret" which has become justly famous: "my Immaculate Heart will triumph." What does this mean? The heart open to God, purified by contemplation of God, is stronger than guns and weapons of every kind. The fiat of Mary, the word of her heart, has changed the history of the world, because it brought the Savior into the world— because, thanks to her Yes, God could become man in our world and remains so for all time. The Evil One has power in this world, as we see and experience continually; he has power because our freedom continually lets itself be led away from God. But since God himself took a human heart and has thus steered human freedom towards what is good, the freedom to choose evil no longer has the last word. From that time forth, the word that prevails is this: "In the world you will have tribulation, but take heart; I have overcome the world" (Jn 16:33). The message of Fatima invites us to trust in this promise.

Joseph Cardinal Ratzinger
Prefect of the Congregation for the
Doctrine of the Faith